LITTLE BOOK OF

PATEK PHILIPPE

First published in 2026 by Welbeck
An imprint of Headline Publishing Group Limited

Text copyright © 2026 Josh Sims

1

This book has not been authorised, licensed or endorsed by Patek Philippe, nor by anyone involved in the creation, production or distribution of their work.

Cataloguing in Publication Data is available from the British Library

ISBN 978-1-03543-293-6

Printed and bound in China

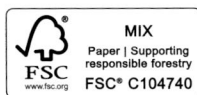

Headline's policy is to use papers that are natural, renewable and recyclable products and made from wood grown in well-managed forests and other controlled sources. The logging and manufacturing processes are expected to conform to the environmental regulations of the country of origin.

HEADLINE PUBLISHING GROUP LIMITED
An Hachette UK Company
Carmelite House
50 Victoria Embankment
London EC4Y 0DZ

www.headline.co.uk
www.hachette.co.uk

The authorised representative in the EEA is Hachette Ireland, 8 Castlecourt Centre, Dublin 15, D15 XTP3, Ireland (email: info@hbgi.ie)

LITTLE BOOK OF

PATEK PHILIPPE

The story of the iconic brand

JOSH SIMS

WELBECK

CONTENTS

A SUPREME LEADER

There are any number of individual reasons why Patek Philippe
might be revered in the world of Swiss watchmaking. But perhaps
the best explanation is that it is rare to find the sweet spot
between so many of those reasons, and Patek Philippe does.

P atek Philippe's watches express, for example, both
technical and aesthetic excellence; the company is a
classical watchmaker but also a pioneer in researching
materials and methods that might move watchmaking forward
in new ways; it's independent and family-owned – giving it
control over its finances and future – and yet also a company
that has nonetheless grown big enough to be able to afford
the investment that this research entails; and it's a globally
recognized and credible watch brand yet one not so ubiquitous
as to have risked losing its air of exclusivity. *Patek Philippe* is not
a name that gets splashed around. It's not one that the company
seeks – perhaps to the cost of its bottom line – to build through
expensive sponsorships or gauche celebrity associations. It has
class. And class is highly desirable.

Indeed, Patek Philippe is a deeply private company, with its
financial and production figures not released, and its output
being just as restrained. While it could sell many more watches

OPPOSITE One of Patek Philippe's most esteemed
complications, the Perpetual Calendar, ref 1518.

ABOVE Thierry Stern, president of Patek Philippe and the fourth generation of the Stern family to run the company.

– 10 times more – the company protects its position at the top by making what is estimated to be a maximum of some 60,000 pieces per annum, with stated intentions to push that number down, not up. It is estimated to have produced fewer than one million watches since 1839 – for comparison, Rolex likely produces close to that number every year.

Likewise, Patek Philippe has never cashed in by producing a sub-line of more entry-level watches. It has even ceased to produce certain references (the codes manufacturers typically give to each version of its various models) altogether when it deemed that they had become too popular and risked overshadowing its other efforts. "I don't have shareholders pushing me to increase [production]," Thierry Stern, the company's president at the time of writing, has told *Forbes*. "If Patek Philippe was a company with shareholders, you would only see the Nautilus today because they'd say 'make a lot of them because it works [i.e. sells]'. And this would kill the company."

Setting its own pace and its own agenda has allowed Patek Philippe to maintain quality control too – Patek Philippe is one of the few companies to design, make and even distribute its watches almost entirely in-house. "[And] we go so far in terms of craftsmanship, development and research that we can't contract these out [anyway]," Stern has argued to *Swissinfo*. While other, greatly respected watchmakers use a machine to finish (that is, decorate its watch's many parts), Patek Philippe finishes all of its parts by hand. Such is its emphasis on quality that the company has introduced its own "seal", surpassing the highly sought industry standard for Genevan watchmakers.

This emphasis also means its production runs are relatively small, from as little as five to, at most, a few hundred of each model, but rarely without importance. Patek Philippe constantly builds on its own heritage with a flow of often historically important refinements to watchmaking – it created the first split-seconds chronograph, the first perpetual calendar and the first annual calendar and has, at various times, held the record for the most complicated mechanical wristwatch ever. As Sandrine Stern, head of creative at Patek Philippe and wife to Thierry Stern, put it to CNN: "Patek Philippe is never easy. Never."

It may take years for these watches to be fully conceived and, for each example, further years to build. Decades may pass before its competitors catch up on their innovations – and these include world-class watchmakers in their own right, the likes of Audemars Piguet and Vacheron Constantin, with which Patek Philippe is said to form a kind of "Holy Trinity" and with which it battles for market share. Yet Patek Philippe introduces a distinctly new model only very rarely. Decades may have passed since the last one. This is a philosophy of less is more, of playing the long game.

A CONSERVATIVE COOL

To some eyes this means an archetypal Patek Philippe watch may appear aesthetically conservative, more classical than contemporary – and the product of a cautious, conservative company which, for good or ill, does not embrace the hype. Those who wish to show everyone that they're wearing a Patek Philippe inevitably lean towards the more visibly identifiable models, the likes of the company's huge hit, the Nautilus. Yet many of its ardent followers see more beauty in its complications (that is, any function beyond displaying the time).

In 2014, Thierry Stern argued that actually there has been a subtle shift with each generation that runs the company: "We've been able to combine my father's [Philippe Stern] very classic culture with my younger ideas [such as using more colour], even though I'm already 53," he said. "[Now] I'm trying to teach my younger colleagues the importance of innovation while staying faithful to the codes of Patek Philippe."

BELOW Patek Philippe's own museum, in Geneva, Switzerland.

It's by combining innovation and tradition that Patek Philippe can keep surprising, he added. "[Just] traditional Calatrava watches – this is not what my sons' [generation] expect. I have to take the best of the traditional and the future and see if they match to make a beautiful watch," Stern told *Hodinkee*.

That the company has followed a relatively restrained, carefully controlled path and made it its own, regardless of trends, is something it has not conceded but trumpeted. In 2009, Patek Philippe put out a statement that serves as a summary of its guiding ethos.

"Every time a new model is developed," it announced, "the key issues are its function as a measuring instrument and the need for easily legible indications. The silhouette of the movement and the integration of its function within a reasonable diameter are the guiding factors as well, because despite the current trend toward ever bulkier wristwatches, Patek Philippe places emphasis on timeless elegance. In the short term, this may not always meet the market's capricious aesthetic preferences, but Patek Philippe knows from 170 years of experience that lasting value can only be created with confidence in matters of style and with deep respect for the principles that define the heritage of watchmaking."

It's a testament to Patek Philippe's sense of history that it claims to be able to repair any of its watches dating back to the founding of Patek, Czapek & Cie in 1839 – it holds some eight million spare parts in stock, some of them over 150 years old, and with each new model adds to its inventory of spare parts to meet estimated needs over the next 50 years. What's more, it displays some of its truly benchmark-setting watches in its own benchmark-setting public museum in Geneva.

That was the brainchild of Thierry's father Philippe Stern, who began collecting Patek Philippe watches for posterity in the 1960s. As he told the Swiss watch trade publication *Europa Star* in 2019, there were bargains to be had at the time: "Back then collectors weren't really interested in wristwatches and you could find them at unbelievable prices." He cited a ref 2410 minute repeater for which he paid 30,000 Swiss francs; the same piece would be a million-plus today.

"In order for anything to be passed on, it must first be kept," he added. "The concepts of conservation and preservation are at the heart of our family business. Throughout all the upheavals history has thrown at us, we have always been careful to keep everything." And he means everything: photos, advertisements, design drawings, bills, models, ledgers documenting every watch it has made – it would be fair to say that Patek Philippe has hoarder tendencies.

All this tends to make a Patek Philippe watch expensive. That is, if an individual shows enough "class" themselves –

ABOVE Inside the Patek Philippe Museum, a treasure trove of the company's historic timepieces.

based not just on their wallet, but their prior purchase history, their influence and so on – to be afforded the opportunity to buy one. It's an approach that may leave the company open to accusations of elitism (and Patek Philippe is not alone among top watchmakers in taking this approach), but with long, long waiting lists, Patek Philippe seems determined to maintain as much quality control over its customers as its manufacture.

Certainly to be a Patek Philippe owner is to be a member of a very special club. And so Thierry Stern was ready to criticize Sylvester Stallone's decision to sell his Grandmaster Chime in 2024 after just a few years of ownership: "It is not fair for a client that may have been waiting for this piece for many years and then sees it being sold," he told *Watchpro*. Controlling who gets a Patek Philippe is "part of the job," he added. "I can be criticized, [and receive complaints] that I have sold a watch to this person or that person, who is then selling it. [But] you cannot control humans one hundred percent."

BELOW An early pocket watch, featuring full enamel landscapes on both sides of its case.

Besides, Patek Philippe is perhaps the only large-scale Swiss watchmaker whose models at least hold their value and invariably increase considerably. Time and time again Patek Philippe watches have set record-breaking figures at auction: of the top five watches to achieve the highest bids at the time of writing, four are Patek Philippes. Among them are a perpetual chronograph, ref 1518 – one of just four examples made in steel – which sold to a private collector in 2016 for US$11 million, and a Grandmaster Chime, ref 6300A-010 – again, the only one of its kind made in steel – which sold in a 2019 charity auction for a staggering US$31.19 million.

All the same, it seems clear that for the company the idea of one of its watches being bought purely for investment – rather than the delight in stylistic, technical and historical accomplishment that they afford – is anathema, counter to

ABOVE Thierry Stern in 2015 speaking during an interview at the Patek Philippe headquarters and manufacturing facility in Geneva, Switzerland.

the tradition and celebration of mechanical artistry that Patek Philippe has come to represent in the world of watchmaking.

Will the next generation to run the family business feel the same? "Their mother and I told [our children] that if they wanted to do something different we had no problem with that at all, because we didn't have children so they could take over Patek Philippe," Thierry Stern has said. "[But] in the end both our boys have chosen to work with me, and I'm very happy about that."

The tradition continues.

LEFT The most complicated watch made by Patek Philippe at the time of its launch, the Grandmaster Chime, here the ref 6300G.

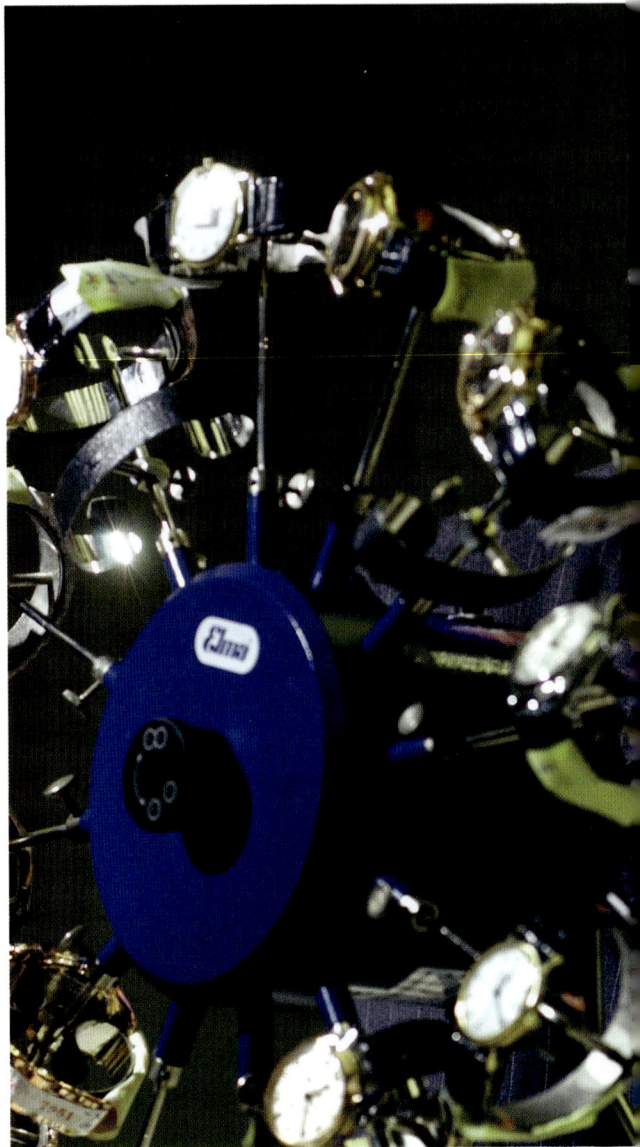

RIGHT Philippe
Stern, Thierry's
father and the
president of Patek
Philippe from 1993
to 2009.

A HISTORY OF PATEK PHILIPPE

THE ORIGINS OF A REVERED BRAND

OUT OF POLAND

There are other Swiss watchmakers that could be considered
more rarefied, more elitist even. Certainly there are others that
are much better known, perhaps others that are considered more
stylish. Yet, among watch aficionados and enthusiasts, Patek
Philippe is a revered, almost mythical name – hugely desirable
for many yet, for most, out of reach. It's the go-to name in historic
haute horlogerie.

Yet, while Patek Philippe has come to be considered
inseparable from Geneva – the Swiss city in which it has
long been based – its origins actually lie in Poland, and
in war. There, in 1830, one Antoni Norbert Patek de Prawdzic
was a young army officer caught up in the uprising against
Russian occupation and fighting for Polish independence.
After two years of conflict, and with the Russian forces having
captured Warsaw, the uprising was considered a lost cause – and
Patek de Prawdzic, together with some 50,000 other insurgents,
fled the country, ending up first in France – where he found
work as a typesetter – and finally in Switzerland.

OPPOSITE Patek Philippe became a front runner in the production
of perpetual calendar watches from the 1920s onwards.

Geneva had by this time experienced its own turbulent times, founding a democratic constitution in 1780, which collapsed a year later, being annexed by France in 1798 and, after the fall of Napoleon, re-establishing itself as a city state and Swiss Canton around 1814. It was also established as a European hub for the making of luxury goods, and of pocket watches especially. It found buoyant demand among both Restoration Europe's aristocratic and rising industrialist classes too.

This allowed Patek de Prawdzic to find new employment as a reassembler – buying in watch movements and cases from various suppliers and having them put together in his workshops. So successful was this business model that soon he was looking for a partner, one he found in Francisek Czapek, a fellow Pole of Czech origin. Together, in 1839 they founded Patek, Czapek & Cie. Over the next five years, the company produced around 200 pocket watches a year – specializing in chronometers – and became a well-established part of Geneva's business landscape, so much so that by 1841 Patek de Prawdzic was able to become a Swiss citizen. He subsequently renamed himself Antoine Norbert de Patek – a name with a less Polish and more Swiss flavour.

A PARISIAN AFFAIR

De Patek and Czapek's working relationship was troubled, but business continued to boom, such that four years later Patek was actively seeking markets abroad, most notably in France, now a more stable country. It was here, at the French Industrial Exposition of 1844, that he met a pioneering 30-year-old Parisian watchmaker, Jean Adrien Philippe, who had just won a bronze medal for a patented innovation he'd come up with two years before. This was a new mechanism for winding a pocket watch's mainspring without the usual, if awkward,

OPPOSITE Antoni Norbert Patek de Prawdzic, co-founder of Patek, Czapek & Cie, the forerunner of Patek Philippe.

use of a separate key. That winder would come to be known in watchmaking as the crown.

De Patek immediately appreciated its potential to streamline the design of his watches, and greatly improve their functionality – so much so that, as soon as his contract with Czapek ended in May 1845, he asked Philippe to become his new business partner. While Philippe did not yet get his name over the door, a new company by the name of Patek & Cie was founded – its premises in Geneva on the banks of the Rhone – with himself, De Patek and a lawyer called Vincent Gostkowski as co-owners.

But Philippe's contribution could hardly be ignored: over the next few years he would radically overhaul the way the Geneva workshop was organized, from single watchmakers hand-assembling single watches, through to what was then considered an extremely modern approach of more specialist individuals working on a production line, using, where appropriate, mechanized tools. The success of that overhaul was undeniable, and on 1 January 1851 the company was renamed again: Patek Philippe & Cie was born.

The two main business partners also established a division of labour for themselves. De Patek put his efforts into sales and building a name for the company, which he did across Europe and the United Sates – where he established what would prove to be a long-term relationship with Charles Lewis Tiffany, of the New York jewellers Tiffany & Co. – winning the likes of the Emperor Franz Joseph I of Austria, Queen Victoria and Pope Pius IX as customers. Philippe continued to head up watchmaking, publishing a book on watchmaking, *Les Montres Sans Clef*, or *Watches Without Keys*, in 1868 – underpinning his already high reputation – and over the following years introducing a series of further innovations.

OPPOSITE One of Jean Adrien Philippe's biggest innovations, first proposed in 1842: a pocket watch that did not require an additional key for winding.

LEFT Patek Philippe has long been one of a few Swiss watch manufacturers to make (nearly) all of its parts in-house.

The year 1868 also saw the company become the first Swiss manufacturer to create a wristwatch – for Countess Kocewicz of Hungary – this being a time when wristwatches were not only a newfangled idea but typically worn only by women – their dress lacking a pocket for a pocket watch – and by women of means at that. (In 1875, Philippe would commission a wristwatch as a wedding present for his daughter Louise, and this would remain the only wristwatch owned – and what's more only temporarily – by either Philippe or De Patek.)

The wristwatch was just one of a series of innovations for which Patek Philippe sought patents over the late nineteenth century and early twentieth century. It was awarded 70: the precision regulator, in 1888; the so-called "perpetual" date display, in 1889, which allowed it to remain accurate without the need for correction regardless of the differing lengths of the months or leap years; the first woman's wristwatch minute repeater, made for one Mrs D.O. Wickham, in 1916, and for whom it would chime the hours, quarter hours and the nearest number of five-minute intervals (allowing accurate time-telling by sound alone); the double chronograph, in 1902; the first split-seconds chronograph, in 1923; the first retrograde perpetual calendar wristwatch, in 1937… And on and on.

TAKEOVERS AND TROUBLED TIMES

The period also saw a change of ownership. In 1877, De Patek died and Philippe was left running the business, which he did until his own death in 1894. At this point the company's employees acquired it, with Philippe's son-in-law, Joseph-Antoine Benassy-Philippe, taking over management and, in 1901, making Patek Philippe & Cie a limited company.

OPPOSITE This simple yellow gold Patek Philippe watch may have been produced to be worn by army officers.

While Patek Philippe would continue to innovate, this new period of ownership did encounter hard times: the New York

LEFT Patek Philippe was innovating the chronograph movements for its watches from early in the twentieth century, this one with Art Deco detailing.

stock market crash of October 1929 – and the Great Depression that followed – saw, inevitably, a huge downturn in demand for luxury goods, which left Patek Philippe and other watchmakers struggling. Jacques-David LeCoultre, the heir to LeCoultre & Cie – one of Switzerland's most successful watchmaking businesses – and co-founder, with Edmond Jaeger, of Jaeger-LeCoultre in 1903, was a close, long-standing supplier to Patek Philippe, so much so that they had a finishing shop in Patek Philippe's offices. He now offered to buy Patek Philippe, an offer that was declined.

Instead, the company managed to stay broadly within employee hands when, in 1932, a majority holding was bought by brothers Charles and Jean Stern – whose own family firm, Stern Frères, were dial-makers for Patek Philippe. This marked the start of recovery for Patek Philippe, but it also marked the end of an era. Joseph Emile Philippe, grandson of Jean Adrien

OPPOSITE & BELOW Chronographs would prove one of Patek Philippe's most desirable complications: the watchmaker created the first double chronograph in 1902 and the first split-seconds chronograph in 1923. Opposite, the Calatrava Chronograph ref 533.

ABOVE A model from 1953, with day/ month, date pointer and moon phase.

Philippe and the last of the owners with a connection to the founding families, lost his stake in the Stern takeover.

The Stern brothers – together with Jean Pfister, previously of the Tavannes Watch Co. as managing director – immediately started to reposition Patek Philippe from being a high-end assembly house to an innovative manufacturer producing its own movements. It now made a series of high-profile steps. In 1932 it was appointed official supplier to the Polish Air Force, an arrangement that lasted throughout the Second World War; in 1943 it produced its first automatic movement; and that same year it joined an elite of around a hundred watchmakers by winning the important chronometer certification for several models from the Geneva Observatory – the official body responsible for measuring the accuracy of timepieces and certifying them as chronometers.

NEW IDEAS – AND CURSES

Crucially, the company also sought to underscore an identity for itself though distinctive designs – starting, most notably, with its 1932 Calatrava, ref 96. Far from being visually fussy or overcomplicated as a means of showing off Patek Philippe's watchmaking credentials – as many watches of the time were – this was instead a clean-cut, almost minimalistic dress watch style of rational, Bauhausian directness.

The Calatrava was a bold move and even, perhaps, a big gamble. But it paid off. The watch became a bestselling style, which would come to be regarded as a calling card for the professional classes and defined a whole new, and widely imitated, category of watch. Further, it alone helped Patek Philippe fend off bankruptcy while the global economy righted itself. It would also epitomize the brand, defining it as one that could offer watchmaking excellence and technical accomplishment together with, unusually, disruptive experimentation.

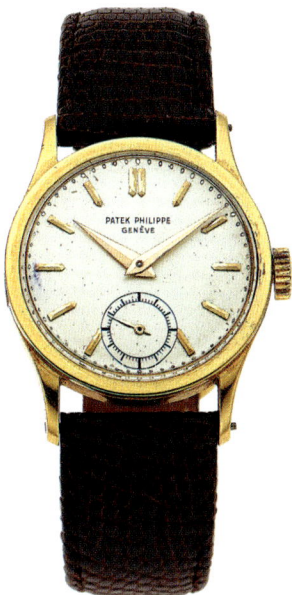

LEFT Groundbreaking for its plain style, the Calatrava, ref 96, was introduced in 1932, this model being from 1937.

Even during times when the wristwatch was fully established as a men's accessory, even during the interwar years of expressive modernity, the company would still make of point of driving home its reputation for expertise in the most unexpected way. After five years in development, 1933 saw the unveiling of – of all things – a yellow gold pocket watch, one priced at US$15,000 and commissioned by the American banker Henry Graves, who had requested an "impossibly elaborate" timepiece.

That is certainly what he got. The pocket watch came with 2 dials, 920 parts and 24 complications, including a minute repeater, alarm, stopwatch with split seconds, moon phase – and the night sky over New York City's Park Avenue. It also showed astronomer's time – tracking the Earth's rate of rotation in relation to the fixed stars rather than the Sun to give a day just under four minutes shorter than usual. All this would make it the most complicated watch in the world at the time – and, remarkably, for another 56 years (until 1989).

The Graves pocket watch would also inspire some fantastical storytelling: it was said to be cursed on account of the owner's best friend dying seven months after he took delivery and then, two years later, his son dying in a car crash. So convinced was Graves, in fact, that there was some connection to the pocket watch that at one point he planned to throw the timepiece into a lake. His daughter stopped him and said she would take the watch off his hands, and her son later sold the watch for US$200,000. In 2014 it was auctioned for a record-breaking US$24.4 million.

COMMERCIAL, AS WELL AS BEAUTIFUL

But the company wasn't just about making exotic one-offs for the super-rich. A few years later, in 1937, it returned to being more practical and commercially minded in producing the likes

OPPOSITE Following its launch in 1933, the Graves pocket watch was the most complicated watch in the world for over half a century.

OPPOSITE
Although
elegant in gold,
the rarest and
most valuable
examples of
the perpetual
calendar ref 1518
came in stainless
steel – only four
are thought to
exist.

LEFT Introduced
in 1940, the ref
1526 was for the
next 12 years the
only perpetual
calendar in
production from
any company.

of the first standard-production wristwatch with a world time function – and in so doing built a reputation for the supreme accuracy of its timepieces. By the end of that decade, in fact, the Geneva Observatory had made some 764 awards to Patek Philippe, accounting for over half of all the awards it had given up until that time. By 1950 Patek Philippe had clocked up 1,728 such awards over the previous half century – almost as many as all other watchmakers had won combined.

Patek Philippe kept the pace up through that post-war period too, following with the first perpetual calendar wristwatch (ref 1526), the first standard-production perpetual calendar chronograph (ref 1518) and the first self-winding perpetual calendar (ref 3448) – a full 16 years before any other Swiss watchmaker would work out how to do it. But it would also come up with stylistically more unconventional designs too, including the 1968 super-slim Golden Ellipse.

Perhaps the best indication of Patek Philippe's progressive attitude – not just as watchmaker, but more broadly as a business careful to hedge its bets – is its establishment of an electronics division in 1948. This meant that the company today most readily associated with excellence in the micro-mechanics of mechanical movements would play a key role in the development of cheap, battery-powered quartz movements that, some 20 years later, would begin to wipe out much of the Swiss watch industry. By the mid-1980s, the workforce had halved and the number of watches made fallen by more than half.

OPPOSITE The Patek Philippe ref 3448 was the first serially produced, self-winding perpetual calendar wristwatch.

In 1952, Patek Philippe launched the world's first solar-powered or "light-wound" clock. The company described it as "a marvel of miniature engineering", explaining that "daily exposure of four hours to an illumination of 200 lux (enough light to permit reading or writing without eye fatigue) will keep the clock running indefinitely." The US market was particularly interested in this latest tech – combined as it was with the company's heritage in micro-mechanical excellence – and Patek Philippe exhibited it at the World Symposium on Applied Solar Energy in 1955 to great fanfare. New York's Tiffany & Co. sold the clocks and prestigious institutions, including the Museum of Science in Boston, acquired one for display.

BELOW & OPPOSITE Although best known for its mechanical wristwatches, Patek Philippe also has a long history of making table clocks, including perpetual calendars and the first to be solar powered.

Patek Philippe's domed solar timepieces, designed by Gilbert Albert with a top that could be swivelled so the solar cells faced the best available light source, would become collectible in their own right, appreciated too for their displays of decorative arts. In fact, these timepieces helped Patek Philippe maintain the skills base capable of such artistry at a time when it was less in demand for watches.

In 1956, Patek Philippe would go on to develop the world's first electronic clock. On the side it would also be building highly accurate electronic timekeeping equipment for industrial use in railway systems, nuclear facilities and airports.

The company's reputation was heading skywards. It would not descend.

THE MODERN ERA

New ownership would also mark the company's transition to what would become another family dynasty. Charles Stern died in 1944, to be replaced as the head of the company by Jean Pfister, but on Pfister's retirement in 1959 Charles' son Henri Stern would become Patek Philippe's president. He was largely responsible for driving Patek Philippe's sales further still in the thriving, post-war United States, which became Patek Philippe's most important market, responsible for some half of all sales over the mid-century decades.

His son, Philippe Stern, would in turn take over his father's role in 1993, his key contribution arguably being to keep Patek Philippe rigorously independent at a time when many watch companies were being subsumed into giant luxury conglomerates, and doubling down on this position with the company's move to a state-of-the-art, purpose-built production facility in Plan-les-Ouates. In 2009, Philippe Stern would be succeeded by his own son, Thierry (still the president of Patek Philippe at the time of writing).

Certainly the ideas of legacy and heritage have remained core to what Patek Philippe is – as its advertising consistently underscores – and the company expects they will continue to be. It's why, as Philippe Stern once explained, the company has maintained a diverse skills base in-house regardless of whether or not there is a need for those skills. The maintenance of legacy, he has said, "happens when savoir-faire [expertise in hand-making] is passed down from one generation of watchmakers to the next, even when it might seem that a specific technology is obsolete and no longer serves any purpose".

OPPOSITE Some perpetual calendar wristwatches expressed Patek Philippe's skill in packing a lot of information onto a dial without it becoming overly cluttered.

PATEK PHILIPPE'S MOST IMPORTANT MODELS AND COMPLICATIONS

STANDOUT MODELS AND COLLECTIONS

Patek Philippe has, to date, never made a connected watch. Aside from the challenging prospect of trying to compete with the likes of Apple, the world of wrist-worn computers just isn't Patek Philippe's: "[We] don't have chips, or quartz... Okay, we have a quartz movement, but we are mostly working with something mechanical, that we can disassemble," as Thierry Stern once stressed to *Hodinkee*. "As a kid I was always working on my bikes, and it's the same. We are preserving a certain manner of mechanics."

B ut within that manner, the company has explored a broad range of expressions, from its best-known and more contemporary sports models, through to its traditional and rare grand complications. As different as these two approaches may be, they are both expressions of style and of substance.

CALATRAVA

"Calatrava" would come to be regarded as a genre of watch in its own right, like "diver" or "pilot". But that genre – simple, unadorned, with a time or maybe time and date-only display –

OPPOSITE A "Padellone" ref 3448 perpetual calendar with moon phases, the distinctive red dot is the leap-year indicator which was added in the mid-1970s.

LEFT This 28mm ref 438 model was first launched in 1935 as a small, sporty watch and was the first from Patek Philippe to have a screw-down casebook for water-resistance.

first belonged to Patek Philippe's 1932 watch, ref 96, even if the name Calatrava would be attached only much later, in the 1980s.

By then the adoption of the Calatrava name for the ref 96 was perhaps recognition of its pivotal place in Patek Philippe's fortunes. It was taken from the cross design used by the Calatrava knights – who held the Calatrava fortress in Spain against invading Moors in the middle of the twelfth century – and had been Patek Philippe's logo since 1887, probably in imitation of fellow Swiss watchmaker Vacheron Constantin's choice of the Maltese cross more than a decade earlier.

Certainly, when the ref 96 was launched the company had a lot riding on its design – it both signalled a new era under the ownership of the Stern brothers and came at a time when Patek Philippe needed a hit to fend off the huge financial pressures of the Depression. And, while Patek Philippe would much later take a broad view on the stylistic elements that would shape its Calatrava line, David Penney's radical design for the ref 96 was certainly precise and distinctive, shifting high-end watchmaking away from the sometimes fussy taste of the preceding Art Deco era – excess ornamentation was often used to signal a watch's prestige and complexity – towards a more compact (at 31mm, some would say small), Bauhaus-inspired rationality. In many ways it was – and remains – the very definition of the modern watch.

The ref 96 was the first round watch in which the lugs were not soldered to the case but flowed uninterrupted from it, curving down to hug the wrist and making it comfortable to wear. It had a slim case and flat bezel. The dial was relatively plain too – using baton markers, Arabic or Breguet numerals and perhaps with a central seconds display, making it highly legible too. In fact, Patek Philippe would make a number of Calatravas for the military – the design might be considered a progenitor of the field watches of the 1940s – and would later apply the term to its own more tool-like watches as well.

Soldiers, however, were not at the time the audience Patek Philippe was seeking. The Calatrava may still have embodied the company's craft: the markings of a seconds sub-dial, for example, were engraved onto the plate and then painted in black enamel and fired, while perle – a machining technique using a diamond drill to give precise consistency – was employed for the minute markers. By 1934 the ref 96 also had Patek Philippe's first in-house wristwatch calibre, or movement, the result of the Stern brothers' belief that the company needed to improve its technical capabilities. This would be the first Patek Philippe watch to be given a reference – a move that helped the specific model stick in consumer's minds.

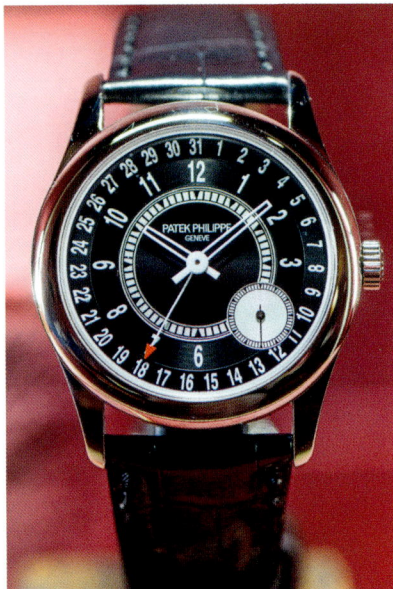

LEFT A Calatrava 6006G with a unique black dial and white numerals, as well as a prominent off-centre sub-dial.

RIGHT About as stripped back as Patek Philippe dials get – the ref 96, this version dating to 1953.

Despite all this, the watch, as it turned out, would be much less complex than the company was used to making and was thus less expensive too. This made it not exactly a watch for Everyman, but at least it was affordable to a rising and aspirational middle-class, with Patek Philippe even making some versions with quotidian steel cases. Patek Philippe was no longer just for aristocrats and industrialists. This broadening of the company's customer base was quickly followed by Patek Philippe's rivals too, each of whom was soon to make their own take on the Calatrava.

Such was the ref 96's success that it was manufactured for some 40 years, going on to inspire many Calatrava variants along the way, most notably the ref 3919 of 1985, with its grooved, so-called hobnail bezel, (back again) soldered lugs and affectionate nickname the "banker's watch" for the way it came to be symbolic of the era's Wall Street-style, more ostentatious displays of success.

JEWELLERY WATCHES

LEFT & OPPOSITE
Designer Gilbert
Albert radically
rewrote the Patek
Philippe aesthetic for
women, introducing
signatures such as
bracelet watches,
as with this model
(left) from 1960,
and asymmetry, as
with this gold ref
3424 (opposite) from
1962.

It's a habit of the Swiss watch industry that most of the designers behind even its most iconic watches remain anonymous, and that's true too for Patek Philippe – with a few exceptions. One might be Gerald Genta, the independent designer behind the Nautilus (see page 65). But before him came Gilbert Albert, the designer who had the greatest impact on the more avant-garde aesthetic of Patek Philippe.

A pupil at Geneva's L'Ecole des Arts Industriels from the age of 15, Albert joined Patek Philippe aged 25 and was soon, by any other name, its creative director. He had found a kindred spirit in the then company boss – the art-loving Henri Stern, who had recently become the second generation of the Stern family to run the business, and who made the case that Patek Philippe was missing a major market in not providing more adventurous watch designs for those customers, at the time mostly women, who were drawn more to a watch's form than its mechanics. "As its performance is enduring," wrote Patek Philippe of one its watches in its 1960 catalogue, "so is its beauty. Technician and designer work together for co-ordinated perfection."

Patek Philippe was wary of the commercial potential of many of Albert's designs – much as some had been about the Nautilus too – and these never made it into production. But Albert had at least persuaded the company to break from tradition – a watch case, he proposed, could be any shape, not just round – and even to reconsider the pocket watch as an object which still had a place in the mid-twentieth century, now reimagined as a pendant watch.

That one series of pendant watches was called the Futuriste, and that in this collection were pieces nicknamed the Television, Meteorite or the Fossilised Leaf – using materials taken from meteorites or fossils – or that in the Ricochet collection was found the likes of the Flying Saucer, suggests just how much part of the new atomic age Albert was in his thinking.

The asymmetric, 18-carat gold Ricochet was described by Patek Philippe in a 1958 catalogue as an "ultra modern vision of the dependable and time-honoured pocket timepiece [pointing] to the fact that no matter what tradition has dictated in the past, there will always be new concepts to be visualised and new channels to be explored in the sphere of design". Then it added, a little apologetically, that a "more conservative collection of pocket models is of course also available". But the awards were a testament to Albert's vision: from 1958 Patek Philippe scooped the Diamonds International Award, at the time the Oscar of watch design, three years running.

ABOVE The Albert-designed Futuriste pocket watch, ref 798, with gold dial made by Stern Frères.

That vision would be extended to wristwatches as well, including the unisex Asymetrie of 1959 – a "glimpse of the future" in rhomboid and triangular shapes – which was utterly unlike anything Patek Philippe had made before. Its production was short-lived, with pieces often made to order. Certainly Albert's heart lay more with jewellery than watches – the heavily textured gold and pearl-set bracelet, ref 3295, from his Tutti-Frutti collection is a case in point – its watch face was hidden behind a flap – and in 1962 he left Patek Philippe to start his own jewellery design firm.

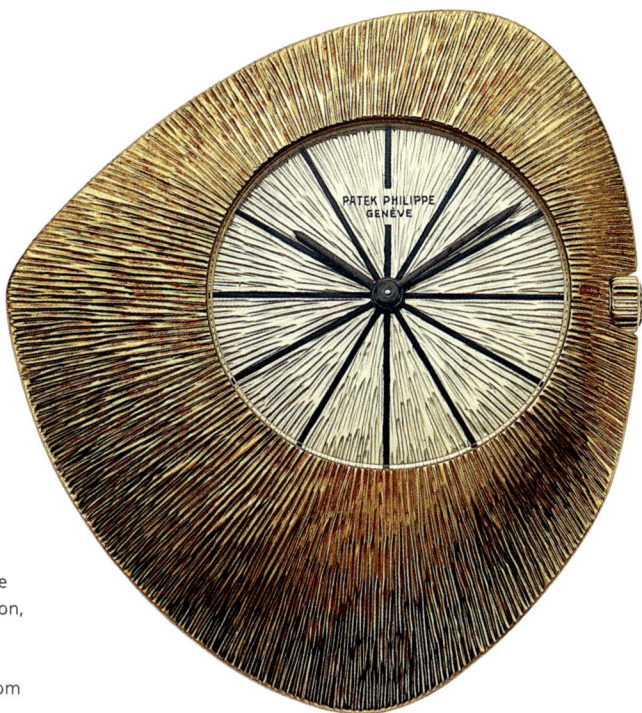

RIGHT Part of the Ricochet collection, the ref 788, was another nature-inspired form from Gilbert Albert.

GOLDEN ELLIPSE

'It is," said Thierry Stern, on the occasion of the Golden Ellipse's 50th anniversary in 2018, "one of those watches that shows you how to make a Patek Philippe. No gimmicks, just purity and beauty expressed through simple design." And, he might have added, some ancient Greek thinking. The proportions of the Ellipse were precisely mathematical, following Euclid's Golden Section, which proposes that the perfect point at which to divide a line into two unequal lengths, such that they still remain harmonious, is to the ratio of 1 to 1.6181. The ratio can also be found, Patek Philippe explained, in nature, in the human form and, for centuries after Euclid, in much classical architecture. Now, in 1968, with the refs 3546 and 3748, it appeared in a watch.

"Having sought inspiration from centuries of aesthetic rule, the designers of Patek Philippe were once again able to rise to a challenge they constantly face. In the Golden Ellipse they found a style which is beautiful and will remain beautiful," as an advert from 1980 puts it.

OPPOSITE & LEFT One of Patek Philippe's most elegant designs, the ref 3546 (opposite), Golden Ellipse with deep blue dial, and the ref 3748 (left), with gold dial.

RIGHT The ellipse shape was used by Patek Philippe not only in the vertical but also on the horizontal plane, to different effect, as with this ref 3545.

Patek Philippe wanted that timeless idealized form precisely because, while it would be made of gold, the Ellipse would be one of the company's most minimalistic of designs: proportionality was front and centre. (In one advertisement it riffed on the use of gold, explaining "Why the value of a gold Patek Philippe goes up even when the price of gold goes down"; in another it accordingly referred to the watch as a "$1700 Trust Fund".)

That proportionality – used here to great effect by Patek Philippe's in-house designer Jean-Daniel Rubeli – also had to make this unisex watch stand out as special at a time when quartz movements were threatening to disrupt the industry with affordable alternatives. In 1983, Patek Philippe would even market the Ellipse as "the non-watch" – as somehow beyond the functional requirements of more everyday timepieces. "People who merely need to know the time will choose a watch – not a Patek Philippe," it claimed.

This would also be the first time in which Patek Philippe would design its own case, to be made by Ateliers Reunis – a company it would later acquire – rather than selecting from a range of case designs proposed by case makers. Nor was this the only experimental step for the watchmaker: the Ellipse's dial would be made of gold, yet rendered blue using a groundbreaking process – developed together with dial-makers Singer – in which cobalt and 24-carat gold were vaporized in a vacuum and then allowed to condense on an 18-carat gold plate.

In another first for Patek Philippe, the Ellipse came with an array of matching accessories. The same blue-gold process was used to make Ellipse cufflinks, tie clips and key rings, as well as Ellipse clocks and pendants. The shape would also be echoed in

BELOW The cufflinks have a less elongated shape compared to the other Ellipse accessories, but it remains popular – it is still sold today, updated in white gold and rose gold.

the form of a Patek Philippe lighter. So successful was the Ellipse – arguably it was key to saving the company from the quartz onslaught that was so devastating to much of the Swiss watch industry – that over the subsequent years the company would produce some 65 different versions, including bejewelled, jumbo, skeleton, one with a brown gold dial (using the same process) and even, in the early 1980s, a quartz-powered, super-slim, sporty Nautilus hybrid, nicknamed the "Nautellipse" (ref 3770).

RIGHT In the early 1980s even the Nautilus was given an Ellipse-style makeover in the form of the hybrid ref 3770, nicknamed the Nautellipse.

OPPOSITE Among the Ellipse accessories, Patek Philippe included this 18-carat gold lighter, made with the same precision found in its watches.

OPPOSITE Gerald
Genta, considered
one of the all-
time great watch
designers here
holding the pocket
watch version of his
Classic Quantieme
Perpetual Squelette
'Harlequin'.

BELOW A sketch by
Gerald Genta of a
design for IWC, with
exposed screws,
akin to his Royal Oak
watch.

NAUTILUS

The legendary independent watch designer Gerald Genta – who created watches such as the Ingenieur for IWC, the Constellation for Omega (as well as the case for its Seamaster), the dollar watch for Corum and the Bvlgari-Bvlgari for Bulgari, among many others – didn't much like wearing a watch.

He once said that he was more intrigued by a nice, comfortable pair of shoes than a watch; that, in fact, he considered the wearing of a watch as something of an irritation. "Watches are the antithesis of liberty. I am an artist – so I hate having to adhere to the constraints of time," he said. "I do really like creating them. Their design for me is a means of expressing my own personality. [But] I don't like wearing watches."

ABOVE The Royal Oak, the watch designed by Genta for Audemars Piguet and launched in 1972.

There were two exceptions, also of his own design, that made it onto his own wrist: an Audemars Piguet Royal Oak (introduced in 1972) and a Patek Philippe Nautilus (ref 3700), launched in 1976 and which he sketched out over a five-minute lunch break during a Basel Watch Trade Fair, while sitting just across from Patek Philippe executives. For Genta the Nautilus especially expressed his golden rule of watch design – "to be classical yet also new at the same time".

"You know, it's very difficult to knock on the door of a prominent company and say, 'This is what I propose you do!' It's very pretentious. It's a delicate situation and you will never be recognised for your talent. I had to wait very patiently [for that]," Genta would note. And patient he was: the Nautilus, like several of his designs, was too radical on its launch – arguably necessarily so, since the mechanical watch market was being crushed by the quartz one at the time – and so initially a commercial flop. Perhaps this was no surprise, even to Patek

Philippe, given that the company was then known as a maker of delicate, complex watches in precious metals. But the company also knew it was out to break the mould.

The idea, after all, had been to offer its first sports watch, one that, stylistically, would "work as well with a wet suit as a dinner suit…or when you set out to slay dragons in the boardroom," as an advertisement of the time put it. But, perhaps more radically still – albeit following the same idea as the Royal Oak – it was also an attempt to position steel as a luxury material. Patek Philippe made no bones about this. It likened its steel to that of a great sword from bygone times. The Nautilus was initially priced at around US$3,100, while an 18-carat gold Patek Philippe watch could be had for around US$4,000.

RIGHT Genta saw no reason to maintain a sense of high seriousness in his watch designs, as this ref G.3622.7 Minnie Mouse model for his eponymous brand suggests.

LEFT & OPPOSITE
Two versions of
arguably Patek
Philippe's most in
demand watch, the
Nautilus, a "Jumbo"
model in steel
(left) and in gold
(opposite) with a bi-
metal bracelet.

PATEK PHILIPPE'S MOST IMPORTANT MODELS AND COMPLICATIONS 69

RIGHT A Nautilus "Jumbo", ref 5711M in gold.

In another advert it even boasted that "one of the world's costliest watches [the Nautilus] is made of steel" – but also that, inside this watch, the "swinging mass" that automatically winds its movement was made of a solid piece of 21-carat gold. The steel only emphasized the overall industrial aesthetic of the watch, with its largely matte finish and porthole-shaped dial opening, flanked each side by a protruding, hinge-like "ear", said to be inspired by those on transatlantic liners. The name itself was a nod to the submarine in Jules Verne's *Twenty Thousand Leagues Under the Sea*.

There was much else that was fresh and challenging about the Nautilus: it had a two-part case for enhanced water-resistance; its bracelet, distinctive for rectangular centre links, was fully integrated, in contrast to most watches then on the market, and its lugs could accommodate alternative straps; the dial itself was blue and had a horizontal ribbed texture, achieved by carving each groove by hand; and then, while the watch had an ultra-slim movement, there was its case's 42mm proportions, generous for the times and earning it the nickname "Jumbo".

By 1981, Patek Philippe had introduced a more accessible, 37.5mm midsized version (ref 3800) – also available in other metals, including rose gold – all in a bid to draw more customers. And over the following years, the company would, of course, produce further interactions, some of which are now considered transitional models – part-way between Nautilus and Aquanaut. But these would merely build on what by then had become an iconic watch, the demand for which seemed to perplex even Thierry Stern. In order to protect Patek Philippe as a whole, he would even take deliberate steps to cool down the overheated demand, especially for the most simple, most cultish, time-and-date-only version, ref 5711. This was made available with a Tiffany blue dial in 2021 before finally being completely discontinued.

Indeed, Stern would once comment that the Nautilus was just one of some 140 models the company was then producing. They were, he told the *New York Times*, "models that are more

BELOW One of the most striking signature details of the Nautilus – its ribbed dial.

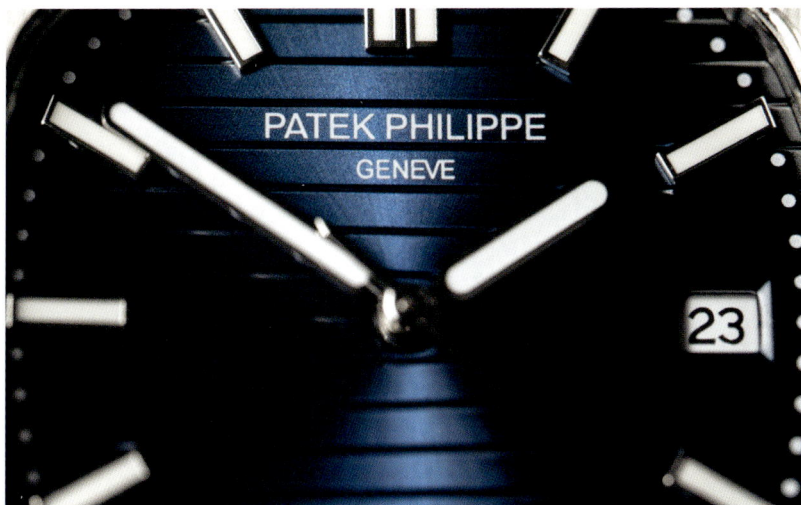

complicated and arguably more beautiful… We cannot put a single watch [like the Nautilus] at the top of our pyramid." That, as it turns out, is precisely where many Patek Philippe fans – and more than a few people who regard it more as an investment or status symbol than an intriguing design – would put it. No wonder Patek Philippe's sports models are said to account for some 40 per cent of its sales (at the time of writing) – Nautilus is just one of its more commercial, contemporary, sportier styles that allow it to keep making its important haute horlogerie pieces.

BELOW A magazine advertisement for the Nautilus, playing on the idea that the watch's shape was so distinctive, its maker's name was not necessary.

These three words do more than identify one of the world's great watches.

They remind you that you are linked with a name that, all through our 142 years, has been the choice of people who have been determining the course of history.

Model shown: Nautilus in two-tones with gold dial. For gents and ladies.

PATEK
PHILIPPE
GENÈVE

Patek Philippe S.A., 41, rue du Rhône, CH-1211 Genève 3

RIGHT A fan
favourite, the
discontinued flyback
chronograph
Nautilus 5980/1R,
with the distinctive
60-minute and 12-
hour counter.

GONDOLO

The idea that the hype which invariably surrounds the launch of a new Patek Philippe model is new is mistaken. Go, for example, back to 1901, when the company started selling some exclusive gold-cased pocket watches through Carlos Gondolo's jewellery shop in Rio de Janeiro, Brazil.

Gondolo's name might have worried Patek Philippe. After all, his father Emilio had actually had a turbulent relationship with the company, not least because of his claiming, in 1869, to be the sole agent for Patek Philippe in Brazil. This forced the company to publish a statement in the local newspaper to the effect that it had "never sent him a single example of their

BELOW Patek Philippe's Gondolo line of watches grew out of a relationship with a dedicated Brazilian retailer.

watches". But a few years years later, it was his son pursuing a new venture, and a new relationship could be forged. In fact, Gondolo & Labouriau – the watch retail business Gondolo would later establish with Paul Labouriau, of a local family diamond business – would in time become one of the busiest retailers of Patek Philippe in the world, at one point said to account for a third of the company's turnover.

Such was the demand for these new timepieces – not least because Gondolo had requested several special technical upgrades on Patek Philippe's already advanced design – that the shop had to run what it called the Plano de Club Patek Philippe System: some 180 watch enthusiasts paid into this subscription plan and every week, for 79 weeks, one of their names would be picked out of a hat to choose who would receive a watch, with the rest of their payments subsequently cancelled. At the end of that time, any less lucky member of the "Chronometro Gondolo" club – or the "Club Patek Philippe", a name Gondolo was smart enough to trademark – would eventually get their watch after paying in full.

The plan made owning a Patek Philippe more feasible, at least for the lucky: the watch was the equivalent of an average annual salary in Brazil at the time. But the hype for the watches was genuine too. Not only did the members of this plan pose for photographs wearing sombreros with the brim turned up – with "Patek" written underneath – but in 1912, a century ahead of rappers singing the praises of Patek Philippe, a composer by the name of F. Santini wrote a celebratory 'Patek Waltz'. "Patek" even entered the Brazilian vernacular as an all-purpose noun for any watch, regardless of whether it was a Patek Philippe or not. Gondolo & Labouriau would run some 118 such clubs until 1913, when a new system was introduced with a draw linked to the numbers published in the state lottery.

Gondolo & Labouriau's relationship with Patek Philippe would last until 1927 – the retailer would go out of business eight years later – but the Gondolo name would live on in a collection launched in 1993, built around Art Deco styling and bringing together most of Patek Philippe's "form" watches. "Form" is the term used for those that are not round but mostly rectangular or tonneau-shaped, and would include the likes of the Patek Philippe Gondolo, ref 5100 – launched in 2000 and recognizable for the triangular, winglike details on the sides of its case – as well as many others given a high jewellery makeover, such as Gondolo Serata, ref 4972, a diamond-clad model with an hourglass-shaped case and a guilloche mother-of-pearl dial.

OPPOSITE A Patek Philippe ref 3733 Gondolo, from around 1979, with a distinctive ribbed case (echoing the Nautilus) and bracelet.

RIGHT The ref 5100J may be Art Deco in style – with those "wing" effects on the case – but it was only launched in 2000.

AQUANAUT

As had been true for the Nautilus before it, Patek Philippe debuted the Aquanaut in 1997 with the intention, at least in part, to reboot its public image as mostly a maker of traditional, visibly luxe, haute horlogerie watches. This time the company wanted to appeal to a market of younger people who were newly wealthy, thanks to the dot.com boom, but who had yet to buy into what they might have perceived as a fusty brand.

The original Aquanaut, ref 5060A, seemed even more utilitarian than Gerald Genta's Nautilus, with its three-part stainless steel case (a later version would give it a record-breaking water-resistance of 120m/390ft for a watch with an exhibition back), large, highly legible, tritium-painted Arabic numbers and – in a first for the company – a "tropical" strap, seemingly made of rubber though actually made of a cocktail of 20 different materials in order to make it bacteria- and UV lightproof, as well as impervious to salt water.

Much as the Nautilus's bracelet form echoed the striations of its dial, so the raised grid pattern of the Aquanaut's strap echoed that of its guilloche dial, in glossy black, the only colour offered at the time. It was in the Aquanaut that Patek Philippe would later use splashes of bold contemporary colour, of which its collection was otherwise devoid.

The Aquanaut was proudly sporty. In fact, the company was said to have started pondering just such a watch after a still anonymous client asked them for a sufficiently rugged wristwatch that could be gifted to his nation's top-flight army officers. Fittingly, that grid patterned dial is said to have been inspired by a hand grenade – or the blocks in a bar of Swiss chocolate. Patek Philippe would tone down this dial effect considerably on later versions.

RIGHT The Aquanaut, ref 5968A, with a self-winding flyback chronograph movement.

Yet the Aquanaut was not aggressively sporty. It had a slim 3.5mm profile and almost contrarian compact size – at 36mm, with a "Jumbo" 38mm version released the same year – running against the 1990s trend for ever larger watches. And with that Nautilus-style port-hole dial shape, this time softer and more of a rounded octagonal, it managed to hit some sweet spot that allowed it also to be worn as a contemporary dress watch.

The nod to the design of the Nautilus initially won the Aquanaut no favours with Patek Philippe purists: just as a Tudor was too readily dismissed as the little brother of a Rolex, so the more affordable Aquanaut was the little brother of the Nautilus, this despite there being no difference in quality. The confusion between the two names was understandable, though.

ABOVE The Aquanaut 5168G, given an outdoorsy styling thanks to a khaki-green embossed dial.

Despite its precious metal and Roman numerals, the Nautilus ref 3800, released in 1996, is often read as proto-Aquanaut, so similar is the design, albeit one that didn't quite go far enough. Enter the better-known version, the ref 5060A, a year later. And even Patek Philippe would continue to refer to this model as both a Nautilus and an Aquanaut for some time – initially even promoting it as part of the Nautilus collection, and sometimes stamping "Nautilus" on the strap's buckle.

The purists would come round to it – such that, to start with, those buying into this new multifunctional model most enthusiastically were established Patek Philippe owners. Those younger first-time customers had to wait. But then, perhaps more so even than the radically steel Nautilus, the Aquanaut came to redefine what a luxury watch could be, in time attracting such customers as Ringo Starr, Paul McCartney – who wore one for his wedding to Nancy Shevell in 2011 – and the investor George Soros.

TWENTY-4

Patek Philippe may have been responsible for some of the earliest women's wristwatches, but for most of its history its output skewed towards men, with women's watches produced as smaller versions of those. It didn't have a standout women's watch – until the advent of the Twenty-4, ref 4910, coming out of extensive research that suggested customers wanted a jewellery watch that was easy to wear but visually strong enough that it was identifiable as a Patek Philippe.

The result, launched in 1999, would be a Gondolo-like, Art Deco-inspired model with a two-tier rectangular case that came in diamond-set steel, a first for Patek Philippe, with a back

LEFT An advertisement for the Twenty-4 model, ref 4910, with a tag line used for women's watches before the "Generations" campaign dominated.

onyx crown and distinctive cufflike bracelet – one that Thierry Stern would describe as "even more powerful than the Nautilus's bracelet". It was powered by an in-house quartz movement, but one far more sophisticated than anything generic. Super-compact, it would nonetheless comprise of 57 parts – some of them decorated – and have six jewels to prevent wear on its gears. Retailing at around US$8,000, the Twenty-4 was also accessibly priced, at least for a Patek Philippe.

So much so, that the company decided the Twenty-4 would probably be considered by its owners to be more of a personal fashion statement and less of an heirloom-in-the-making, and that including it in the then still young "Generations" advertising campaign would not be appropriate. Instead, photographer Glen Luchford shot a top model, Bridget Hall, for an image that ran with the relatively cryptic tag line "Who will you be in the next 24 hours?" The success of the Twenty-4 led to a rapidly

BELOW The round, automatic Twenty-4, with a sunburst dial and bezel set with diamonds.

expanded collection of versions in rose or yellow gold, with ever
fancier gem settings, an automatic movement and, in 2006,
another dedicated advertising campaign, this time riffing
on "Generations", stating that, "You don't just wear a Patek
Philippe. You begin an enduring love affair."

The Twenty-4 would also prove groundbreaking for the
company in creating awareness of the brand among women, and
with a growing interest in mechanical movements, this paved
the way to offer, from 2011 to 2012, complications including a
dedicated a split-seconds chronograph, ref 7059; minute repeater,
ref 7000; and perpetual calendar, ref 7140.

CUBITUS

When Patek Philippe launched its Cubitus model, ref 5821, in
2024, this was its first major new sports watch in 28 years. Yet
while the design had an obvious pedigree, sharing aesthetic cues
with both the Nautilus and the Aquanaut, it was sufficiently
controversial that when images of a complication version of the
new watch spread online – taken from an advertisement in *Fortune*
magazine that ran ahead of the launch – some commentators even
questioned whether it was real.

Others accused it of being too much like its predecessor designs
– with its ribbed dial, and with even the name "Cubitus" (which
Patek Philippe had registered long before it was assigned to any
design) echoing that of the Nautilus. This despite the fact that, as
before in Patek Philippe's story, the Aquanaut was originally also
launched as a Nautilus spin-off. Others considered the Cubitus to
be some kind of outlier. This, note, was also Patek Philippe's first
sports model launch in the opinionated age of social media.

It even sparked enough animosity in the watch press that
Thierry Stern was prompted to point out – on the Zurich business
site *Bilanze* and in his characteristically outspoken way – that
"haters are mostly people who have never had a Patek and never

will have one." On another occasion he is said to have told one journalist that he was well used to people telling him in a meeting how much they hate a new model, and then trying to reserve one for themselves on the way out…

Meanwhile, others loved it, with horophiles picking up on the fact that one particular version, ref 5822, with its asymmetric sub-dials, was one with an entirely new display for Patek Philippe: an instantaneous grand date with six patents to its name and one which would change within 18 milliseconds. Too fast, in other words, to see it happening.

For others the Cubitus was testament to the scrutiny that the decisions of a historic company like Patek Philippe come under, especially from passionate followers – and inevitably the Cubitus became a bestseller, one increasingly appreciated precisely for its own distinctive, square-but-slim, identifiable-at-a-distance shape. Patek Philippe had made many square and tonneau-shaped watches before – the likes of its Art Deco-style Gondolo Cabriolet, ref 5099, for example, or the Gondolo, ref 5010 – but the Cubitus was arguably the company's first square sports model, or rather one that "blends the square, the circle and octagon," as the company would describe it.

Given that the vast majority of watches are round – and given that this is what most customers want – the Cubitus's bold shape was a bold move commercially speaking. And, at the time of writing, its long-term success is yet to be proven. After all, Patek Philippe had created another sport watch before and then quietly discontinued it: the Neptune, ref 5080, was launched in 1996 as being "ideal for sportswear", and in many respects it pre-empted the mania for steel sports watches that would follow. But perhaps it was too ahead of its time – "the supremely elegant Neptune is, at the same time, the perfect dress watch" and was taken out of production just six years later.

OPPOSITE Patek Philippe's Cubitus 5821 model – dividing the brand's fans, despite, or maybe because of, its clear lineage from the brand's previous sports models.

CALIBRE 89

To call the Calibre 89 a pocket watch is perhaps to stretch the truth. It is, after all, at 9cm (3½in) across, more the size of a carriage clock, and weighs around 1.1kg (2lb 7oz), so is not, strictly speaking, a practical timepiece. What it was, however, when it was unveiled in 1989, was the most complicated watch in the world, and the most complicated for 26 years. It would remain the most complicated too, until 2015, when watchmaker Vacheron Constantin created its ref 57260.

In its sizeable, 18-carat gold-cased form, the Calibre 89 houses a triple spring barrel movement with a non-visible tourbillon, offering 33 complications, among them world time for 125 cities; perpetual calendar – which could also display information such as the moon's passage, star chart and day/night indicator; times of sunrise and sunset; a grande and petite sonnerie with carillon – a mechanical chime; a minute repeater; split-seconds chronograph; compass; hydrometer; thermometer; barometer; altimeter…

By way of a notched programme wheel – which advances one step per year, each step having a different depth – it also displayed the "moveable feast" that is the date of Easter. This complication is widely considered to be the single hardest one to devise, and it has not been duplicated since (at the time of writing).

Indeed, so hard is it – not least because Easter, unlike, say, a leap year, does not fall in a set pattern over a short number of years, but only over many years – that the Calibre 89 was able to display that date accurately only until 2017, at which point the programme wheel needed to be replaced with one for later years. In contrast there's a reason why the watch's perpetual calendar shows not just day, month and year but also the century – because it's accurate up to the twenty-seventh century.

OPPOSITE The Calibre 89, unveiled in 1989 and, at the time, the most complicated watch in the world – albeit one sized more like a clock.

A boon to astronomers who are interested in distant celestial objects, the Calibre 89 could even display sidereal time – time measured according to the position of the so-called fixed stars (rather than the Sun), a sidereal day being the time between successive passes of vernal equinox crossing the prime meridian and lasting precisely 23 hours, 56 minutes and 4.1 seconds.

To make all that work required 1,728 components arranged in the Calibre 89's 28mm-thick form over four levels. It also sparked the development of a silent flywheel to regulate the rhythm and duration of each gong strike – thus finally preventing the buzzing background sound that had long blighted chiming watches. Small wonder that the Calibre 89 took nine years to make, and that only four examples in different precious metals were made.

A testament to its complexity, and the required precision in the making of its parts, it was also the first timepiece that Patek Philippe designed using computer-aided manufacturing software. The project was placed under the charge of Jean-Pierre Musy, then a 28-year-old engineer, rather than a through-and-through watchmaker, and later the company's long-standing technical director. It would be his name, along with two others', that appeared on the patent for that Easter date display.

Why did Patek Philippe make such a timepiece? To mark its 150th anniversary – but, of course, the Calibre 89, as much as it would struggle to fit comfortably into anyone's pocket, also expressed the company's superiority in complex watchmaking.

SKY MOON TOURBILLON

The Sky Moon Tourbillon, ref 5002, was the most complicated wristwatch that Patek Philippe had created when it was launched in 2001, and would remain so for 12 years when it was replaced by the elaborately engraved ref 6002. This

OPPOSITE Patek Philippe's ref 5002 double-sided, 12-complication Sky Moon Tourbillon, launched in 2001.

double-faced watch – Patek Philippe's first for a wristwatch – looked relatively conventional with the white dial-side up, which nonetheless starts to express its 12 complications. These include a perpetual calendar and minute repeater, the two complications with which Patek Philippe is most closely associated, the latter in this case comprising cathedral gongs that wrap nearly twice around the circumference of the movement and which – very unusually for the time – were made of an alloy especially developed with the Swiss Federal Institute of Technology.

But flip the Sky Moon Tourbillon over and the reason for its name is revealed: there you see a deep blue, starlit night sky – featuring Sirius and the Milky Way – as a canvas for displaying standard time, sidereal time and the phase and orbit of the moon. In doing so the watch came to be seen as the wrist-worn take on the Star Caliber pocket watch, with its complex sky chart, launched the year before in order to mark the new millennium.

Patek Philippe would describe the watch as "a work of art with the heart of a complex scientific instrument", one that might also inspire the same feelings of the sublime as looking up at the night sky. This watch could be, it said, no less than "a window opening onto the mysteries of the universe, inciting us to become, in turn, philosopher, sage, and connoisseur of beauty."

But the Sky Moon Tourbillon was also a nod back to the "Packard" double-sided astronomical pocket watch. Considered to be Patek Philippe's first "grand complication", this was commissioned by James Ward Packard, the American engineer, luxury automobile magnate and inventor of the steering wheel, and was delivered to him in 1927 – sadly in the hospital where he was on his deathbed. The watch featured a rotating celestial map of 500 gold stars, depicting the night sky over Packard's hometown of Warren, Ohio.

GRANDMASTER CHIME

When the Grandmaster Chime, ref 6300, was launched in 2016 – after nine years in development – it became the most complicated watch in Patek Philippe's collection. And, maybe, since it had 20 complications – including a leap year cycle, second time zone, instantaneous perpetual calendar, moon phase and four-digit year display, to name a few – that was hardly surprising. So packed with functions was the Grandmaster Chime that the company's engineers designed what they called "isolators", to block certain operations while others are in use.

To provide all this required packing in 1,366 components, and another 214 in its reversible case, for which Patek Philippe, for the first time, would also design and patent an easy-to-use rotation mechanism built into the lugs. But, as this watch's name suggested, the most celebrated of its complications involved sound – its grande and petite sonnerie, alarm, minute repeater and so on.

This made the watch the culmination of a fascination held by Patek Philippe since 1839, just a few months after the company was founded, when it took an order for a quarter repeater (a pocket watch that chimes on the quarter hour). By 1845, when it sold its first minute repeater pocket watch, Patek Philippe was gaining an industry-wide reputation as the leader in the manufacture of chiming timepieces, and in 1916 it created the first repeating wristwatch – a five-minute repeater, which used two different chimes to strike the hour and then chime the number of five-minute intervals since the hour. In 1939 it upped the ante on this complexity by producing the first minute repeater in combination with another complication, in this case a moon phase and perpetual calendar.

While the complexity of minute repeaters meant they would never be made in large numbers – only seven Grandmaster Chimes would be produced, for example, and one of those was

for Patek Philippe's own archives – they would remain part of the company's regular output, albeit facing a decline in demand through the 1960s and 1970s, in the face of the rise of quartz movements and a shift towards watches that were aesthetically striking over mechanically complex.

Arguably Patek Philippe rebooted interest in the latter with the creation of its Calibre 89, and the vast amount of scientific research that went into making that celebratory timepiece, in mechanics but also in acoustics, fed into several important watches. Among these were the likes of the first automatic minute repeater, made possible by designing an off-centred winding rotor, which left more room for a minute repeater mechanism and other complications – a tourbillon minute repeater, ref 3939, and the Grandmaster.

The Grandmaster would introduce its own patented innovation in chiming watches, an instantaneous date repeater: this allowed the watch to chime not just the time, but also the date. At the push of a button, one double-ringing chime, sounding high-low, would indicate the tens of the day of the month, if required, followed by a single high tone to indicate the units.

WORLD TIME

Since the world is divided into the 24 time zones established by the International Meridian Conference – held in Washington in 1884 and setting the prime meridian in Greenwich, UK – there is a clear benefit offered by a watch that can be calibrated to show the correct time wherever in the world its wearer is. That had long been the thought of Emmanuel Cottier, a watchmaker who first proposed the idea to the Société des Arts in Geneva in 1885 – to very little interest – and then to his son Louis who, in 1931 devised and filed a patent for the mechanism that would allow the simultaneous display of the time across those 24 zones.

OPPOSITE One of Patek Philippe's most complicated wristwatches, the Grandmaster Chime, ref 6300, and also one of its most aesthetically extravagant, coated in 409 baguette-cut diamonds.

OVERLEAF Patek Philippe created the first world time watches in 1937. This 1963 model, with two crowns, ref 2523, sold for more than US$1 million at auction in 2012.

Cottier initially worked on his concept with a watchmaker by the name of Baszanger, whose dials were made by Stern Frères – who acquired Patek Philippe in 1932. Thus it was Patek Philippe that would get to run with the idea, creating the Heure Universelle watches, ref 515R – the first world time watches – in 1937, launching them and soon many other iterations into an era in which luxury long-distance travel was coming into its own.

These set a design template – place names from around the world, each in one of the time zones, set on a fixed and later a rotating bezel, with a separate 24-hour ring that could be set to correspond correctly to a.m. or p.m. – which would form the basis of Patek Philippe's much more complex World Time watches over the following years, including the World Time, ref 5531, which was revealed in 2017 to mark the company's 175th anniversary – with an enamel centre dial depicting the skyline of Manhattan. This too was a nod to a traditional Patek Philippe World Time aesthetic: earlier models, starting with the ref 605, might feature a cloisonné enamel dial, a technique by which the

BELOW Despite its elaborate design, the Minute Repeater World Time watch, ref 5531R, is just 8.5mm thick.

outlines of the continents are marked out using thin gold wire, and the area inside each is then filled with a different coloured enamel to create a world map in miniature. Others might feature instead a motif more personal to the timepiece's owner.

Some aspects of the past would necessarily be left behind, however. Many place names from earlier World Time watches had since changed, with some becoming less important, others, like Saigon, Peking and Bombay, having become defunct and yet others, such as Bagdad, showing now outmoded spellings; these older models consequently give an intriguing insight into the travel interests and geopolitics of their time. But the gist of the idea of the World Time watch would remain.

Geopolitics would play out in other ways too: before the Second World War, London and Paris were in the same time zone, but the occupying Germans forced the French to adopt Central European Time. Patek Philippe made the leap of faith that the Allies would prevail and the previous arrangement would be restored. But while they did, it wasn't – leaving some models of the pre-war and war period out of step with the reality after 1945.

PERPETUAL CALENDAR CHRONOGRAPH

If there is one complication – among the many it has mastered – that might be most closely associated with Patek Philippe, it is the perpetual calendar chronograph. The idea may not have been Patek Philippe's own – it was probably the British watchmaker Thomas Mudge, who in 1762 first proposed a timepiece that automatically adjusts its date display to allow for variations month to month, taking into account leap years too. But the complexity of the Mudge pocket watch was enough that any other watchmaker was dissuaded from taking the idea further until Patek Philippe co-founder Jean Adrien Philippe experimented with it for pocket and pendant watches from the 1860s.

Certainly by 1925 Patek Philippe was the global forerunner in the development of this kind of movement, not least by putting one inside a wristwatch, ref 97-975, and by the 1930s a regular production of perpetual calendar watches only confirmed the image of Patek Philippe as maker of the most advanced movements on the market. Indeed, this set the path for the

BELOW A yellow gold perpetual calendar chronograph, ref 2499, introduced in 1941 and often considered to be one of Patek Philippe's most beautiful watches.

periodic launch of reported advances on the concept over the next 30 or so years, often by extensively modifying a Valjoux calibre 23 movement, one which would find its way into timepieces by several leading watchmakers, Vacheron Constantin and Audemars Piguet among them.

In 1941, the ref 1518, for example, set out what would become a signature dial configuration for the brand, with twin in-line apertures for the day and month indication at the 12 o'clock position, as well as date indication and moon phase on a sub-dial at the 6 o'clock position. The ref 2499 was launched in 1951 (with the series discontinued in 1985) and is often considered simply the most beautiful of the "Holy Grail" perpetual calendar chronographs, examples of which have been owned – and sometimes sold on at auction – by celebrities such as Eric Clapton (a Patek Philippe super-fan), Jay-Z and Ed Sheeran. The ref 3448, launched in 1962, was the first automatic wristwatch with a perpetual calendar, while more unusual versions include the ref 3970, with a "TV-shaped" dial and cushion case.

ANNUAL CALENDAR

LEFT An advertisement for a Patek Philippe annual calendar watch, a complication of its own design launched in 1996.

When Patek Philippe introduced its first annual calendar watch, ref 5035, in 1996 – a complication that automatically indicates the date for months of 30 and 31 days and which needs to be corrected only once per year, to allow for the variable length of February – this was a testament not just to the company's watchmaking skill but also in some sense its imagination. For anyone concluding that all complications had by the mid-1980s already been made – for all that they may have been constantly refined – here was something original.

As Patek Philippe would call what would become one of its flagship complications – appearing in versions from Calatrava, ref

5396, to Advanced Research ref 5250, to Nautilus, ref 5726 – the annual calendar was a "useful complication", somewhere between an ordinary calendar with the drawback of needing correction five times a year, and a perpetual calendar which is entirely self-correcting, but with the drawback of being an extremely complex and costly piece of engineering.

That there might be a market for a more practicable and affordable complication was something the rest of the watchmaking industry appears to have overlooked – and it was affordable, in part, because Patek Philippe developed a new calibre, in conjunction with final year students at the Geneva School of Engineering. It was based on a rotary stack of gear wheels positioned between the base movement and the dial – comprising a 24-hour wheel that moves a 31-tooth date wheel forward one notch each day, with, at the end of a 30-day month, a second part stepping in to advance the wheel two notches, thus bypassing the 31st. Crucially, this relatively simple system did away with the cams, racks, levers and springs required in a perpetual calendar.

LEFT From Patek Philippe's Advanced Research department, this white gold annual calendar, ref 5250, was launched in 2005 and was the first model to use a Silinvar silicon escape wheel.

LEFT & OPPOSITE
The ref 5035R – in
platinum (left) and
in gold (opposite) –
was the world's first
self-winding annual
calendar wristwatch,
requiring adjustment
just once a year.

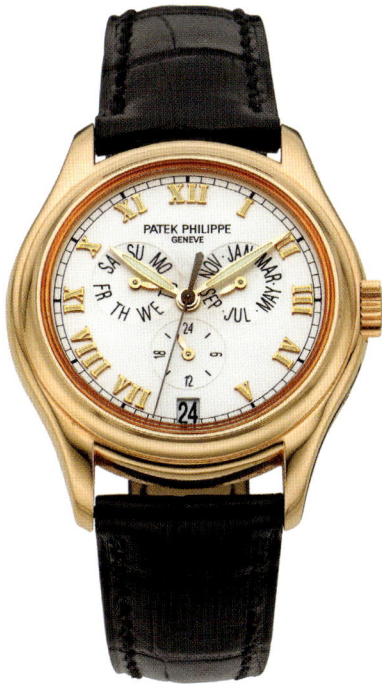

But Patek Philippe also saw the production of this new complication as a way of addressing the tough business climate of the early 1990s, not least a consequence of more watchmakers moving upmarket, producing more complications and somewhat diluting their sense of exclusivity – a trend that had encouraged Patek Philippe to scale back its own production. What the market needed, it concluded, was to plug the gap between everyday and elite watches, thus also creating a gateway product into the world of high complications. The patented annual calendar was as much a brilliant marketing move as a technical accomplishment – one that created a new category of watch and which would later be imitated by many other watchmakers.

OVERLEAF A minute repeater pocket watch dating to 1917 – a technology later hugely reduced in size, but not complexity, so as to be housed in a wristwatch.

MINUTE REPEATER

Much like the perpetual calendar, Patek Philippe did not invent the minute repeater. That complication dates to watchmaker Daniel Quare's invention of 1686 and – in times lacking instant electric light – benefited from its ability to, on demand, sound the hours, quarter hours and minutes, repeating the increments through mechanical chimes. The first movement to use coiled wire gongs – still the template for the minute repeater today – was pioneered by Abraham-Louis Breguet. But arguably Patek Philippe was the company that both perfected the complication and came to be most closely associated with it.

OPPOSITE Launched in 1993 and produced until 2009, the ref 3939 minute repeater tourbillon was one of the few Patek Philippe models to have an enamel dial, by Donze, with Breguet numerals.

BELOW A minute repeater pocket watch dating to 1917 – a technology later hugely reduced in size, but not complexity, so as to be housed in a wristwatch.

In the year of the company's inception, 1839, it was commissioned for a quarter repeater pocket watch. Six years later, the first minute repeating version was launched. But the challenges of both scaling down the 100-plus parts of a minute repeater movement, fitting it alongside other complications and producing an audible, resonant, high-quality sound – all in a much smaller volume – meant that it wouldn't be until 1916 that Patek Philippe unveiled its first repeating wristwatch, a five-minute repeater. Four years later came Patek Philippe's first minute repeater wristwatch and then, another four years later, its first production of a minute repeater wristwatch. One of these was sold to Ralph Teetor, the blind industrialist and inventor of first a fluid-operated gearshift and then, in 1945, of cruise control.

Despite its technical achievement, the minute repeater remained a niche interest, for many perhaps a defunct product given that electric light and luminescent paints meant that a watch could now be visible at night. But Patek Philippe's future president Philippe Stern clearly had a love of the complication, as from 1982 to 1989 he commissioned two examples for himself – though as much to ensure that the company's ability to make such timepieces was not lost. Precise know-how regarding the manufacture of the necessary miniature gongs had, in fact, largely been lost, and only through tapping the specialist knowledge of one particular watchmaker, Henri-Daniel Piguet – of watchmakers Victorin Piguet & Cie – was much of it saved.

Perhaps it is this experience that, in 1989 – Patek Philippe's 150th anniversary – inspired Stern to revive its manufacture, now more as an expression of the company's watchmaking know-how. First came the minute repeater perpetual calendar, ref 3974, following up in 1993 with a minute repeater with tourbillon, ref 3939.

OPPOSITE The ref 3974 minute repeater perpetual calendar was launched in 1989 to mark Patek Philippe's 150th anniversary and was, for a time, the world's most complicated wristwatch.

PATEK PHILIPPE AND THE
SCIENCE OF WATCHMAKING

INNOVATION FIRST

The idea of Patek Philippe is so embedded in the history of Swiss watchmaking and, of course, it has been responsible for countless innovations, each of which has advanced the reliability, precision and occasionally the aesthetics of its watches. Over its history it has filed over 100 patents, and at least 20 of those have been considered groundbreaking in terms of advancing mechanical timepieces, and in many instances Patek Philippe has successfully translated an experimental idea, expressed through a one-off or limited edition watch, into a series/production model – itself almost as great a challenge.

To give just a few instances of the company's many achievements: in 1860, it introduced a winding crown for its pocket watches, replacing a separate key; in 1925 it was the first watchmaker to offer a perpetual calendar wristwatch; in 1937 it produced the first retrograde perpetual calendar and co-produced the first world time wristwatch, ref 515; in 1941 it created the first perpetual calendar wristwatch in series, ref 1526; it came up with the first perpetual calendar chronograph in 1941, ref 1518, and the sweep-seconds perpetual calendar wristwatch, ref 1591, in 1944, and then serially produced this new complication in 1951.

OPPOSITE The ref 1518 was the first serially produced
perpetual calendar chronograph, even if only
281 examples were ever made. History and rarity
guaranteed multimillion dollar bids at auction.

In 1949 the company developed the Gyromax balance, which was patented in 1951 and allows for fine adjustment of the movement without requiring tinkering with the delicate regulator mechanism; in 1962 it introduced the first wristwatch with a perpetual calendar and automatic winding, ref 3448; in 2000 it revisited the world time concept to develop a mechanism that allows for the setting of 24 cities and time zones using a single pusher. And on and on…

Yet if, for all that, the largely classical styling of Patek Philippe's watches might suggest that it is a traditional, conventional, historically minded company, that notion was decisively countered in 2005, when it launched its Advanced Research project. This is a department dedicated to exploring new technologies and materials and their potential application in watchmaking – and works in collaboration with Swiss scientific bodies including the Institute of Microtechnology at the University of Neuchatel, the Geneva School of Engineering, Architecture and Landscape, the Swiss Centre for Electronics and Microtechnology and the Federal Institute of Technology Zurich, among others – and it marked the first time that Patek Philippe began to wear its innovator mindset on its sleeve.

The results have made it into special edition Advanced Research watches (and, later, into some production ones). These have made use of one or several technologies developed by Patek Philippe: the likes of 2005's Advanced Research Annual Calendar, ref 5250, for instance, of which just 100 examples were made, featured the first escape wheel made of a silicon called Silinvar; and 2011's Advanced Research Perpetual Calendar, ref 5550, which had a new kind of balance set-up, the Oscillomax, an assembly of Spiromax hairspring, Pulsomax escapement and GyromaxSi balance spring.

OPPOSITE Launched in 1944, the Patek Philippe ref 1591 was the first water-resistant perpetual calendar wristwatch.

SILINVAR ESCAPE WHEEL

In 2005 Patek Philippe – in conjunction with the Swatch Group, Rolex and the Swiss Centre for Electronics and Microtechnology – developed a new kind of escape wheel, a critical part of the escapement, which controls the release of energy from the mainspring and which is critical to the precision of a watch. Rather than the standard steel, it was made of an oxidized mono crystalline silicon.

What advantages did this bring over steel? For one, it was much harder than steel so was more resistant to wear, and was corrosion-resistant. It couldn't be magnetized – so, unlike steel, wasn't negatively affected by magnetic fields. It was very lightweight relative to steel – which means both that it needed less energy to function and was less sensitive to the effects of gravity. It was highly flexible, remaining perfectly concentric and, because it was made using a process used in the microchip industry called Deep Reactive Ion Etching, didn't need finishing or polishing afterwards. Perhaps most importantly, while steel reacts to changes in temperature – which diminishes the balance wheel's effective function – this crystalline silicon material was stable over temperature extremes. Hence its name Silinvar, a combination of the words "silicon" and "invariable".

SPIROMAX BALANCE SPRING

In 2006 Patek Philippe debuted the first balance spring made from Silinvar in its Annual Calendar, ref 5350. The balance spring – attached to the balance wheel – was invented in 1675, with subsequent improvements coming only rarely, in 1795 and 1895, when it was first made from Invar, a nickel-iron alloy. Making one from Silinvar provided many material benefits, but Patek Philippe concluded that even then it would be subject

OPPOSITE The ref 5905 flyback chronograph annual calendar, one of Patek Philippe's most successful models when it comes to bridging both sports and dress watch styling.

to the effects of gravity over time, causing it to expand and contract asymmetrically.

The company consequently devised what it called the "Patek Philippe terminal curve", a patented way of making the outer end of the spring thicker, which forces it to oscillate concentrically without the need (as another less elegant solution might propose) to use an overcoil instead. As well as being mounted in an innovative way that makes for easier and more consistent manufacture, the so-called Spiromax spring was also three times thinner than previous Invar springs, allowing for the development of super-slim movements.

It first appeared in Patek Philippe's annual calendar, ref 5350, of which only 300 were made. But when the Aquanaut Travel Time watch, ref 5650, was released in 2017, the Spiromax balance spring had been improved further still, by adding an end curve to its inside, which further helped it to counter the impact of errors caused gravity.

Chronometers – supremely accurate, rigorously tested watches – are certified as such by Contrôle Officiel Suisse des Chronomètres (COSC), which demands accurate timekeeping within a tolerance of -4 to +6 seconds per day. Remarkably, Patek Philippe's tiny change to the balance spring meart its watch could be regulated to be accurate to within -2 and +1 seconds per day. That's the same tolerance range expected of a tourbillon – an advanced horological mechanism that seeks to counteract the effects of gravity by rotating the escapement and balance wheel within a cage, and which is respected for its extreme precision.

PULSOMAX

The Pulsomax would be the first escapement made entirely in-house by Patek Philippe and first appeared in the annual calendar, ref 5450, released in 2008. It was a combination of

OPPOSITE The Advanced Research annual calendar ref 5350R, released in 2006 as a limited edition of 300 pieces and housing the Spiromax balance spring.

an escape wheel and pallet fork – a small lever that engages with the escape wheel – made of Silinvar, together with the Spiromax hairspring. This offered several advances, among them no need any longer for the grinding, fixing and adjusting of the rubies from which the pallet fork was usually made, and an enlarged pallet fork – which meant it spent less time in contract with the escape wheel – which overall made the Pulsomax 15 per cent more energy-efficient. This allowed the power reserve (how long a watch will run without rewinding) to be extended from 45 to 60 hours.

ABOVE The movement inside the ref 4550P automatic annual calendar wristwatch, with the exhibition window stating its Advanced Research pedigree.

OSCILLOMAX

The Oscillomax was an ensemble of technologies first seen together in Patek Philippe's perpetual calendar, ref 5550, of 2011. This was significant in that it was the first time Advanced Research tech had been applied to a perpetual calendar – previously it had been seen only in less complex annual calendar watches. So much of a leap was the Oscillomax that it resulted in the application of 17 patents, the most significant of these being GyromaxSi, a modification of the Gyromax balance introduced back in 1949.

Now it was made from Silivar with two 24-carat gold weights added to towards its outer edge. That improved its efficiency by maximizing its moment of inertia between oscillations. But the balance was also now given an hourglass

RIGHT The ref 5550 from Patek Philippe's Advanced Research division, with Oscillomax silicone escapement.

shape that actually made it more aerodynamic – showing just how forces we might associate with much larger machines also apply at the micro-mechanical scale. The lack of aerodynamism of the previous Gyromax, it had been discovered, meant that when it oscillated it lost 60 per cent of its energy due to air resistance. The new shape solved that engineering challenge, and allowed for another jump in power reserve to 70 hours.

FORTISSIMO MINUTE REPEATER

Not all of Patek Philippe's twenty-first century technical advances have been towards improving the efficiency of its watch's time measurement. In 2021 the company unveiled its Advanced Research Fortissimo, ref 5750, of which just 15 examples were made. This was a watch that revised how a minute repeater – which also chimes the time – would be made, in order for its sound to be that much clearer and more audible. In fact, if a typical minute repeater might be heard 10m (33ft) away, the Fortissimo's chimes could be heard 60m (197ft) away.

How did Patek Philippe achieve this? The basis of this minute repeater is traditional: hammers strike a gong that spirals around the movement. For the Fortissimo, a floating sound lever absorbs the vibrations before they reach the case – a desirable result in high-end watchmaking – but a sapphire crystal plate amplifies the sound, funnelling it towards four openings in a titanium hoop at 3, 6, 9 and 12 o'clock. Since this plate is separate to the movement, the case material – which can have a deadening effect in more traditional minute repeaters – has no influence on the quality of the sound, so Patek Philippe made the Fortissimo's case out of platinum, the metal that historically has been most problematic in this way.

OPPOSITE The Fortissimo Minute Repeater, ref 5450P, revolutionized the audibility of watch chimes.

PATEK PHILIPPE IN POPULAR CULTURE

THE CELEBRITY STATUS SYMBOL

It seems the greats of jazz got there first. For all that wearing a Patek Philippe has, for many a contemporary celebrity, become an expression not just of horological knowledge but also of horological one-upmanship – a Patek Philippe watch being less widely recognizable than, say, a Rolex – the avant-garde were wearing the company's watches back in the 1920s.

L ater, Ella Fitzgerald wore a platinum and diamond bracelet watch by Patek Philippe, the brand chosen also by watch enthusiast Oscar Peterson and Count Basie, who wears his on the cover of their 1978 joint album *The Timekeeper*s. Both of the men received theirs as gifts – Basie a Calatrava, Peterson a Patek Philippe in rose gold – from the jazz impresario Norman Granz. When Basie died, Granz bought the inscribed watch again, at auction, as a gift for Peterson.

Duke Ellington, meanwhile, bought his watch at Patek Philippe's Geneva store in 1948 – this is known thanks to the company's laboriously detailed archives – opting for a split-seconds chronograph, ref 1563, one of only three known. The company paid US$1.6 million at auction in 2014 for the same

OPPOSITE American TV presenter – and enthusiastic horophile – Ellen DeGeneres wearing her Nautilus.

"The 1
COUNT BASIE M

keepers"

OSCAR PETERSON

PABLO 2310-896

LEFT Jazz legends Count Basie and Oscar Peterson on the cover of their aptly named album *The Timekeepers* – both had recently been gifted Patek Philippe watches and became lifelong fans.

watch, which is now one of the 3,000 or so watches held in Patek Philippe's archive and/or on display in its Geneva museum.

Certainly a Patek Philippe has long been considered more of a connoisseur's choice. Baseball hero Joe DiMaggio wore one, as did Albert Einstein. Or take John Lennon's Patek Philippe, a 40th birthday gift from his wife Yoko Ono, worth US$25,000 and said to be the only serious watch he ever owned.

Therein lies a tale. A ref 2499, it was one of only 349, making it one of the most sought-after and valuable Patek Philippe watches. After his untimely death just two months later in December 1980, that gold Tiffany-stamped perpetual calendar was long thought

LEFT John Lennon, wearing the Patek Philippe watch given to him by his wife on his 40th birthday – and which sparked a mystery after the Beatle's untimely death.

by Ono to be in the ex-Beatle's apartment in The Dakota in New York. It was allegedly stolen in 2005, passed between auction houses, changed hands multiple times and finally became the subject of a long-running lawsuit between Ono and the man who claimed legal ownership of the watch, according to Forbes.com.

Name-dropping in rap songs has indicated that a brand has become part of the zeitgeist ever since 1986, when Run-DMC sang their appreciation for 'My Adidas', and in 2017 – when, arguably, there was a spike in interest in watch collecting, caused by social media – one in eight of the songs on the *Billboard Hot 100*'s hip-hop chart mentioned Patek Philippe.

Far from Patek Philippe pushing to be recognized, it seems that this younger, more current audience went out and – like those jazz greats before – discovered the brand itself: move over Rolex, the typical rap watch name-drop of choice, step aside Richard Mille… As G4 Boyz' Ice Baby would note: "Rolex is nice, but I could be going to the club and next thing you see somebody else with the same watch. But the Patek Philippe – it's rare. It's different."

Yet the first mention of Patek Philippe in lyrics may have been in 1986, when British prog rock band Emerson, Lake & Powell's song 'Touch and Go' namechecked the brand as symbolic of the lifestyles of the elite, commenting on those living on the street having nothing, including a Patek Philippe.

At the time, understanding that Patek Philippe reference arguably required a genuine interest in high-end watches – and perhaps revealed Emerson, Lake & Powell's own spending habits. If Patek Philippe was mentioned, this was precisely because it signified belonging to exclusive and more elevated circles. In David Fincher's 1997 film *The Game*, Michael Douglas's character is forced to pawn his Tiffany & Co.-stamped 1930s Patek Philippe to just about cover the cost of a ticket home. "With a watch like that, a man doesn't have visa problems," the pawnbroker notes.

Indeed, when Tony Soprano gifts his cousin a white gold and diamond Patek Philippe annual calendar ref 5037 in a 2002 episode of *The Sopranos*, the brand was considered an oddball choice because of its lack of resonance with a mainstream audience (even if it clearly resonated with watch fan James Gandolfini, who played Soprano). Certainly, relative to Rolex, Patek Philippe's appearances in films have been rare and typically used in an attempt to signal something particular about a character, other than just their bank balance: in the 2011 film *Drive*, for example, Ryan Gosling's troubled getaway driver wears what is purported to be his father's vintage Calatrava (or, in actuality, since the film involves many stunts, one of the number of fakes).

OPPOSITE Ryan Gosling plays the Driver in *Drive* (2011), wearing the Calatrava that the character is said to have inherited from his father.

RIGHT James Gandolfini as Tony Soprano in *The Sopranos* (1999–2007), a Rolex fan who in one episode makes a major statement by giving his cousin a white gold and diamond Patek Philippe, ref 5037.

But by the later 2010s and beyond, more ostentatious wealth display would be back on the agenda, with Patek Philippe top choice for that flex. Travis Scott, Cardi B, Jay-Z and Beyoncé, DJ Khaled and Lil Uzi Vert were just a few of the performers who would rap their appreciation, Lil Uzi Vert even releasing not one but two tracks – 'Patek' and 'New Patek' – dedicated to his favourite watchmaker. The American rappers 21 Savage, Metro Boomin and Offset – who mentioned Patek Philippe 15 times across the 10 songs on their collaborative album *Without Warning* – even rapped about their Patek Philippe ref 5790, a watch so rare that it doesn't actually exist.

LEFT The American rapper Lil Uzi Vert – two of his released singles are devoted to Patek Philippe.

RIGHT Actor Mark Wahlberg in his Patek Philippe World Time Date, ref 5330G, on a denim leather strap – just one of many Patek Philippes in his collection.

For many, Patek Philippe's credential as a traditional old money brand – given its long pedigree and high prices – made its more recognizable sports models the perfect choice for the expression of their new money power. That Patek Philippe was the world's most expensive watchmaker, at least by auction records, no doubt only added to its cool. At least, for some. One rapper, Pusha T, would rap about how other rappers' apparent obsession with the brand had spoiled it for him.

Yet if owning a Patek Philippe once suggested a kind of trailblazing, soon just about every star of the stage, screen and music business would be photographed in theirs, from Paul McCartney to Ed Sheeran, TV presenter Ellen DeGeneres to singer-songwriter and keen horophile John Mayer, as well as actor Mark Wahlberg, the owner of multiple Patek Philippes. Often their choice was the Nautilus – but that didn't mean their watch couldn't be special: Drake wore a custom emerald-encrusted version, ref 5726, designed by fashion designer Virgil Abloh.

When Sylvester Stallone spoke with Sotheby's about why he was selling a number of his watches through the auction house, he was particularly admiring of his several Patek Philippes. "The 5711. What can I say? This is the one that started the whole Nautilus movement, [in this case] the first time they used diamonds on steel," he said. "So if you're a serious watch collector and you want to make a statement, this one doesn't whisper, it screams. It's the Mac Daddy. I don't know why I'm selling it? Because I'm stupid I guess."

Well, not quite the Mac Daddy, as he conceded. Also in his collection was an unworn double-faced Patek Philippe 6300G Grandmaster Chime. "When the time came for me to say 'What is the finest watch in the world? I'd like to own that', I said, 'This is it'. And this is not easy to come by," he explained with a smile. "I had to appeal to certain powers that be, write many letters to the board and eventually it was determined that I was going to be the the owner of one of these magnificent pieces of art. This is available only to certain customers, so you have to be with [Patek Philippe] for a while. You're not going to be able to walk in off the street and say, 'Hey, I'd like one of those.' No."

OPPOSITE Paul McCartney waves while wearing his Aquanaut.

LEFT Sylvester
Stallone in his Patek
Philippe Nautilus
– the actor was
also the owner of a
Grandmaster Chime.

THE MARKETING OF
PATEK PHILIPPE

Unmistakable

Golden Ellipse and 18 kt. blue colored gold. They invariably identify Patek Philippe designs. They tell you that the watch was finished entirely by hand, in the manner practiced by Patek Philippe since 1839. The Golden Ellipse was derived by Patek Philippe from the Golden Section, the principle which already inspired the design of the Parthenon. The blue colored gold of the dial is a bit of alchemy signed Patek Philippe.

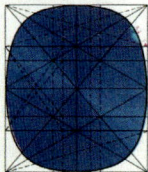

Diamond-set ladies' model (Ref. 4382). Gents' bracelet watch (Ref. 3848/1). Also featuring the Golden Ellipse and blue colored gold are the cufflinks and keyring.

PATEK PHILIPPE
Ennobled by the craftsman's touch

MESSAGES THROUGH MARKETING

In 2015, when *The Atlantic* magazine asked professionals in the advertising industry what they considered to be the best advertising campaign of all time was, Tim Calkins, professor of marketing at Kellogg School of Management, posed this question in reply: "How do you sell a $25,000 watch when people can buy an accurate one for $10?" For him, the best campaign came from Patek Philippe.

L
aunched in 1996 and conceived by the British advertising agency Leagas Delaney in their first work for Patek Philippe, the long-running "Generations" campaign featured images of fathers and sons sharing a special moment. (Photos of mothers and daughters would become a consistent part of the same campaign only from 2014.) In the earlier renditions it would not be clear what watch was being worn, or that anyone was wearing a watch at all. That didn't matter, because this wasn't really about the product – that was what other watch brands did in their advertising. Patek Philippe's famous tag line? "You never actually own a Patek Philippe. You merely look after it for the next generation."

OPPOSITE An advertisement for Patek Philippe's Golden Ellipse, complete with the cufflinks and key ring that the company produced as part of the collection.

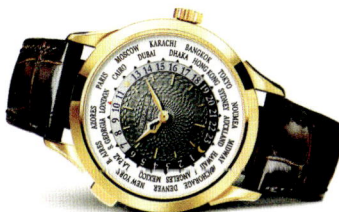

PATEK PHILIPPE
GENEVE

Begin your own tradition.

You never actually own
a Patek Philippe.

You merely look after it for
the next generation.

World Time Ref. 5230R

LEFT Arguably the single most successful – and longest-running – watch advertising programme, "Generations", with its famous tag line about ownership.

Of course, most people will never own a Patek Philippe. But the idea here was clear: not just that a Patek Philippe is built to last, but that it will be imbued with such emotion by its wearer that it inevitably becomes an heirloom. There was another message here too: while many people might collect high-end watches, and these people would certainly know about Patek Philippe, most people will buy just one, if at all. So they had best make theirs a Patek Philippe. The campaign spoke to those who aspired – however they aspired less to a certain brand but simply to have the best.

Indeed, the idea came about as a consequence of Leagas Delaney speaking directly to the kind of people around the world who might conceivably buy a Patek Philippe. "We did one to one interviews with people, often very high-end people who won't talk in a group setting," Tim Delaney told the *Hodinkee* watch publication. One such sets of interviews was in San Francisco. The core of the campaign's idea – initially conceived as the line "Begin your own tradition" – came to him on his flight back to London.

Here was an idea that wasn't just a break with rather conventional watch advertisements featuring a good-looking watch worn by a good-looking person, Delaney argued, but a bespoke fit for Patek Philippe too. "This company, the way they make products, the sense that they're not faddish, that the family is day-to-day involved, and that the "Generations" campaign alludes to a compassionate feeling about potential clients" could, he would argue, hardly work with any other watch company. Importantly, the campaign had a specific emphasis too: "We've never once used the word 'luxury' with Patek Philippe. They're not in the 'luxury' business – they're in the watch business."

Initially, not everyone liked the "Generations" campaign, despite its images being shot by world-class photographers of the likes of Peter Lindbergh, Glen Luchford and Peggy

OPPOSITE Initially Patek Philippe did not include mothers and daughters in its "Generations" campaign, though its message would prove just as effective when it did.

You never
actually own a Patek Philippe.
You merely look after it for the
next generation. *The new ladies' Neptune.*

Hand crafted, with 114 diamonds

set in 18 carat solid gold.

PATEK PHILIPPE
GENEVE

Begin your *own* tradition.

Sirota. Though some praised it, others thought it cheesy and sentimental, at odds with the hard mechanics and performance of watchmaking. Ten years after its launch, the campaign was finally recognized by winning the Prix Suisse de la Campagne Horlogère de L'Année – the Swiss watch advertisement of the year award – despite by then already being well-established as arguably the most effective campaign in watchmaking history.

Certainly, prior to "Generations", Patek Philippe had taken a more predictable route with its marketing, underscoring more the technical accomplishment of its watches. Yet these were so futuristic at the time that it felt it necessary to spell out their merits in a way that would be self-evident to a watch enthusiast today. One 1960s advertisement for its acclaimed perpetual calendar, ref 3448, for example, described it as "The Watch That Thinks". "Automatically," it goes on, "with no need for the owner to correct it for long or short months, it shows the time, the day, the month, the date (even in leap year) and the phase of the moon – and it never has to be reset." The price at that time? What today sounds like a pleasingly affordable £1,285.

By the early 1970s, Patek Philippe had not exactly stopped championing its mechanical pedigree: it had even started to organize what it called Watch Art exhibitions around the world, to show off the finest examples of its watchmaking from its archive. But with increased knowledge of mechanical watches perhaps making blunt explanation unnecessary, at least to anyone likely to buy a Patek Philippe, the company's marketing subtly changed tack, with a new focus more on the whole watch, in both its aesthetic and symbolic value: "A Patek Philippe doesn't just tell you the time. It tells you something about yourself," one advert had it.

OPPOSITE Patek Philippe has rightly prided itself on its vertical integration – from mechanics to decoration, almost everything is done in-house.

OVERLEAF Although steeped in history and tradition, Patek Philippe has nonetheless proven itself to be progressive in technology and its application.

Beyond genius
Patek Philippe's legendary legacy

Every century produces men and women who, through their exceptional achievements, leave an indelible mark on the universe - none more so than Albert Einstein, physicist, humanitarian, true genius.

SOME DISCOVERIES HAVE COMPLETELY altered our lives: electricity, the telephone, the motor car. Although useful, they are minor in their importance when compared to the work of Albert Einstein. His theories have altered forever our views on matter, time, space and motion and have helped scientists across the globe understand our universe.

At 12, bored and frustrated with formal education, the German-born Einstein devoted himself to solving the mysteries of the world. 1905 was his miracle year. Just 26 years old, he conjectured that everything in the universe is a repository of energy. His famous E=mc2 formula theorized that converting a small amount of mass would release an enormous amount of energy (later demonstrated by the atomic bomb). That alone would have been enough to secure his reputation in history.

Yet he published work on critical opalescence which answered the age-old question of why the sky is blue. His general theory of relativity was the first major new theory of gravity since Isaac Newton's more than two and a half centuries earlier. He proved the existence of atoms, modeled the behavior of the entire universe and developed quantum theory.

An outspoken and political man, Einstein was subject to savage verbal attacks and death threats, not only for his political views on pacifism and Zionism, but also for his scientific ones. Just how controversial his work was considered is revealed by the Nobel Prize awarded to him in 1922, not for relativity but for his work on photoelectric effects.

Before Einstein, physicists had always viewed time as immutable. Einstein wore a constant reminder that he was the first to introduce time into the relativity equation. His Patek Philippe pocket watch, with its extra large Roman numerals to compensate for his bad eyesight, was certainly well-worn throughout his lifetime.

After physics, peace became Einstein's most important concern. Having moved to the US in 1933 to escape the Nazis, Einstein reluctantly set his pacifist views aside to write to President Roosevelt in 1939 and urge America to develop an atomic bomb before Germany did. His opinion contributed to Roosevelt's decision to fund what became known as the Manhattan Project. When the atomic bombs were dropped on Hiroshima and Nagasaki, Einstein hoped it would "intimidate the human race into bringing order into its international affairs, which without the pressure of fear, it would not do".

He later considered his letter to Roosevelt one of his greatest mistakes. One of his last acts, a week before his death in April 1955, was an agreement that his name should head a manifesto urging all nations to give up nuclear weapons. "The release of atomic power has changed everything except our way of thinking... the solution to this problem lies in the heart of mankind. If only I had known I would have become a watchmaker," he lamented.

Albert Einstein in 1922, the year he won the Nobel Prize for his work on photoelectric effects

EINSTEIN WORE A CONSTANT REMINDER THAT HE WAS THE FIRST TO INTRODUCE TIME INTO THE RELATIVITY EQUATION.

The company would even write to its dealers to explain how this represented "a milestone in the history of Patek Philippe" in being "the first time [it] presents watches as well as jewellery items in the same ad... It no longer dwells on the technical aspects of the watch but presents it as a hand-finished jewel in its own right, as something that transcends a mere watch."

The same decade had seen Patek Philippe hint at its celebrity associations. One early advertisement to promote the new Nautilus pointed out that its reputation for making "the finest watches in the world [was] a fact borne out by our clientele. Royalty, film stars, composer, authors; in fact celebrities of all kinds have appreciated the perfection of a Patek Philippe." But by the 1980s it started to promote that association with the famous more directly still: "Tchaikovsky's timepiece was a Patek Philippe," noted one advertisement. "Einstein's timepiece was a Patek Philippe," another stated simply, under a photo of the great physicist's watch. Both adverts had a note pointing out that the watch wasn't actually for sale but "other classic styles from the current collection can be seen in our latest brochure."

Of course, advertising is also myth-making. While it cannot lie, it can exaggerate. Consumers know it's bought and paid for. Maybe this was some part of the incentive behind Patek Philippe's decision in 2009 to leap beyond such promotion with the creation of something more reliable and real: the Patek Philippe Seal.

The company had had an association with the Geneva Seal – the Poinçon de Genève – since its creation in 1886, essentially as a marketing campaign to promote Geneva's watching quality, with watchmakers submitting their watches for inspection and certification. But by 1925 Patek Philippe was almost the only company using the Geneva Seal – though this in itself provided an opportunity to stand apart from the crowd – and would remain so until late into the twentieth century when the

OPPOSITE With such a historic fan base – Tchaikovsky wore a Patek Philippe, as did Albert Einstein – the company was wise to brag occasionally.

watchmakers Cartier or Roger Dubuis would make use of it.

By then, Patek Philippe had also reached a stark conclusion: that, in fact, while it had long promoted the Geneva Seal as the ultimate stamp of approval, its own manufacturing standards now far exceeded that of the Geneva Seal anyway. This was, not least, because the Geneva Seal would not recognize expertise beyond the boundaries of Geneva, which had proven to rule out even some of Patek Philippe's most groundbreaking pieces. More strangely, given that watchmaking is in large part all about reliability and precision, it made mechanical performance an optional test. Meanwhile, COSC – the official Swiss chronometer testing institute – was only interested in the precision of the movement, not the whole watch.

The logical step for Patek Philippe was to create its own certification. As it would explain in its advertising, its own seal – represented by a "PP" stamp, typically on a movement's winding rotor – was "a quality benchmark… [an] emblem of horological excellence [that] goes beyond any existing standards of the Swiss watch industry. Uniquely, the Patek Philippe Seal applies to the completely assembled watch as delivered to the owner." The seal, it would add, also "represents a commitment to lifelong servicing and restoration of all timepieces created by us since 1839. [The seal] guarantees the enduring quality of our timepieces. [It is] further evidence that we will never compromise the integrity of our watches."

That promise of lifetime serving was a first for the Swiss watch industry, and while there is no independent external verification – other than the risk to reputation – the Patek Philippe Seal is said to have also set a higher benchmark for reliability and precision than COSC.

OPPOSITE A simple statement – about Patek Philippe's impact on watchmaking history – but hard to argue with.

PATEK PHILIPPE HAS LEFT A DEEPER IMPRESSION ON THE HISTORY
OF WATCHMAKING THAN ANY OTHER WATCH.
10 ROCKEFELLER PLAZA, NEW YORK, N.Y. 10020

CONCLUSION: THE GREATEST, AFTER ALL

Thierry Stern once told *Hodinkee* that what he liked most about his family's company, Patek Philippe, was the "feeling that you are making something useful and nice for the world". Indeed, while Stern would underscore that nothing Patek Philippe made was "gimmicky" – every innovation had purpose – and that certainly its products also expressed a kind of beauty, his statement surely understates the company's contribution, both to the story of watchmaking and, perhaps, to the culture at large.

While it's true that few people will ever have the pleasure of owning a Patek Philippe, that doesn't stop the watches having a significance beyond simple consumerism. Whoever is wearing it, or not, a Patek Philippe watch remains an artefact that not only captures particular and increasingly rarefied craft skills, but which also embodies a specific mindset: the value of creating for posterity.

LEFT Patek Philippe's global retail network has helped make its name famous even to those with little interest in watches.

RIGHT Patek
Philippe at the now
defunct Baselworld
international watch
trade show in Basel,
Switzerland, in 2010.

INDEX

CREDITS

The publishers would like to thank the following sources for their kind permission to reproduce the pictures in this book.

Alamy: A.Astes 82; /Adsr 72, 81, 100, 140, 150; /Associated Press 20, 30-31, 32, 38, 45, 50, 87, 94-95, 155; / Entertainment Pictures 131; /Gacro74 12; /David Grossman 154; /Keystone Press 42; /Malcolm Park 24; /Maximum Film 130; /PA Images 64; /Rapisan Sawangphon 73, 79, 80, 84, 114; / Michael Sikorski 10; /Sipa US 65; / Tubray Media 66; /UPI 89, 104l; / The Advertising Archives: 141-142, 153; /Antiquorum Auctioneers: 41; / Bonhams: 77; /Bridgeman Images: Reuters: 50; /Collectability.com: 54xs; /Getty Images: Bettmann 26-27; / Michael Buzholzer/AFP via Getty Images 15; /Gianluca Colla/Bloomberg via Getty Images: 8; /Fabrice Coffrini/ AFP via Getty Images 48; /John

Lamparski/Getty Images for Roc Nation 132; /Luke MacGregor/Bloomberg via Getty Images 14, 146, 148-149; /Ethan Miller/Getty Images for Cirque Apple LLC 135; /Kayla Oaddams/WireImage 133; /Andreas Rentz 136-137; /John Shearer/Getty Images for MTV 125; / David Wong/South China Morning Post via Getty Images 13, 74; /Jonathan Wong/South China Morning Post via Getty Images 16-17; /Bob Gruen: 128; / Heritage Auctions/HA.com 35, 56, 57, 58, 59, 60, 61, 63, 102, 103; /K2luxury: 92; /© Phillips Auctioneers LLC: 6, 33, 39, 43, 53, 55, 76, 97, 101, 105, 106, 117, 119; /Private Collection: 126-127; /Public Domain: 22; /Shutterstock: Matthew Bain Inc 68, 69, 70; /Rustic and Watches 71; /Sandro Campardo/ EPA: 34; /Stephen Ferdman 52; / PHLD Luca 67; /Martial Trezzini/EPA-EFE 98; /Solanaptosui via Wikimedia Commons: 28; /Sothebys: 62, 118.